The 72 Amazing Ways To Internet Profit

(Second Edition)

Patric Chan

Internet Mastermind Sdn Bhd (783170-V)
1-3-22 eGate Commercial Complex, Lebuh Tunku Kudin 2, Gelugor 11700,
Penang Malaysia
Email: helpdesk@patricchan.name

ISBN: 978-983-44389-2-0

DISCLAIMER: Restricted To Internet Marketing
Techniques, Ideas, And Tactics Based On Personal
Observations And Experience Only.

CONTENTS

ACKNOWLEDGMENTS

This book would never have been written if it weren't for these people I appreciate:

It was a long journey since the day I quit my job at the age of 21, never to be employed again. But it seems like almost yesterday.

For those who believe in me — My dearest Mother for being with me through the hard times of falling when I was doing the best I could. Thanks for believing and caring for me, Mom.

To my Dad for doing your best to bring up your son and teaching me about the lessons of life and how to live a meaningful one. And to my two elder brothers, Chee Wai and Chee Meng for supporting me, unconditionally.

My valuable customers and subscribers for inspiring what I do. If not for them, I would have never strived to be hungry for continuous improvement and the passion to teach people how to create wealth.

Definitely not to be missed, my fellow friends and family members who probably still have no clue what I do for a living, for sharing their happiness, laughter and joy.

And saving the best for the last— my loving wife, Emily Khoo: Someone who's always by my side to cheer and support me when I'm down and remind me not to be a big head when I am at the top. Thank you for your trust, love, work and the happiness that you bring into my life.

ABOUT THE AUTHOR:

Patric Chan's "rags to riches" story has inspired thousands around the world to tap into the internet opportunity.

He has been featured in newspapers many times and also business magazines. Having built his internet empire (without the benefit of any college or university qualification), Patric has taught his techniques and strategies to thousands of his students through his books, courses, seminars and live training.

Patric's internet marketing products and courses have been endorsed and promoted by internet marketing gurus around the world – proving the quality and the value that he delivers. His latest product, The CB Passive Income was one of Clickbank's top seller products when it was launched.

As a very much sought after speaker, Patric has already spoken in 12 countries including United States, UK and Australia as an authority on the topic of internet marketing before he even reached 30 years old. He has also spoken in business conferences alongside presenters from industrial giants like Google, IBM, etc.

The other 2 best-selling books he has authored include WakeUp Millionaire and Clicking Cash, which is co-authored with New York Times best-selling author, Robert G. Allen.

To date, Patric has received testimonials from ordinary people whose lives he has changed and international bestselling authors, millionaires… including a billionaire.

For more details about Patric Chan, please visit **www.patricchan.com**

ABOUT THIS BOOK

The first edition of the 72 Amazing Ways To Internet Profits was published back in 2012.

The one you're reading right now is the 2nd edition – an updated version that compiles many techniques and ideas I've discovered to make me rich online. Wealthy. They are not in any particular order because this is not an encyclopedia type of book. Neither is it a book about how to get website traffic.

Whether you just want to start or are already marketing online, I'm sure you'll get the most out of it.

If you want an A-Z book of internet marketing, this is NOT IT. What you get here are my personal experiences and observations that are proven to work.

There's a reason why I did not write a complete encyclopedia of internet marketing book for you to read. It's simply because I know the content in the 72 Amazing Ways To Internet Profits will be far more valuable than learning the technicality of doing it — **what you want are the concepts and ideas to be RICH.** If you want to learn how to setup a webpage, there are many IT classes and books to show you how.

Do you want to learn how to prepare a burger to sell or how to make a burger business wildly profitable? You know the answer.

In it, I share with you my philosophies of real business building, tricks to get traffic, how to get your website visitors wanting to buy your products, ideas for market research, how to build a mailing list, product creation tips, how to make money online without your own product and a lot more.

Like I said, these are the cool stuff that makes you money, not teaching you how to become a 'worker'.

But if you really need to learn A-Z of internet marketing, don't worry, because I've got that handled for you.

Just go to www.patricchan.net/affiliatemarketing.

You'll learn how to get started, to make your first $100.

Now — when reading this book, you'll notice several topics mentioned repeatedly but with different ideas. Topics like niche marketing, list-building, affiliate marketing, product creation, joint venture, pay-per-click, etc. I have emphasized more of these because of their importance for your online business success.

After reading this book, I want you to be clear on 2 things:

The first one is you won't make a single cent online if you don't apply what you read. I know that discovering new money-making information is fun and exciting but doing them is what sets you apart from the other readers.

The second point is this — Internet marketing is definitely an ongoing education. This book alone will not give you all of the information you need. Come on, be real.

As a matter of fact, I'm STILL LEARNING. I think I'm spending more money now learning compared to before I started making money online. Sounds ironic, doesn't it? Hmm. Not really. Here's why -- because I already know how to create income from the internet, I would make more each time I improve my knowledge and apply new internet marketing techniques I've never used before.

Wait.

There's actually one more favor if you don't mind -- If you like what you have read or gained value from it, I would appreciate tremendously if you can drop me an email with a testimonial or feedback.

Please do this for me by emailing **pa@patricchan.name.**

To your internet success,

Patric Chan
Best-Selling Author, The 72 Amazing Ways To Internet Profits

INTRODUCTION

I've been marketing on the internet since the year 2003. Over more than a decade online, I have experienced my fair share of successes and failures on the internet.

I'm fortunate to have made good money to live the life I wanted before 30 and traveled to 11 countries to speak on the topic of internet marketing and online business.

I've taught thousands of people around the world and with your acknowledgement, I would like to share with you the ideas and techniques that have brought this internet wealth to me in this book you're reading right now.

Just in case you need to run a quick check on me, feel free to use Google.com and search for "Patric Chan". I would understand. Since there are many people out there teaching 'how to make money online,' it's really hard to distinguish a snake oil salesman from a genuine teacher.

Or if you want a quick reference, just go to www.patricchan.name.

I mean, look, there are people who make ten bucks and start shouting like Chicken Little about the falling sky. The next thing you know, self-proclaimed internet 'gurus' start 'popping up' like fresh mushrooms after a rainy day to run seminars teaching others how to make money online. What can you say -- this is a free country.

I make money online by selling mostly info products - educational and 'how to' products in many different topics.

Call them any name you want but they are purely informational products that can be delivered in almost any kind of format such as books, CDs, email courses, DVDs, etc.

But the best ones I like are digital downloadable products.

Customers pay. They download.

That's called autopilot income.

But most of the techniques, ideas and tactics here can be applied to selling other types of products as well – just use your creativity to fit them in.

TESTIMONIALS FROM AUTHORS, INTERNET MARKETERS AND OTHERS AROUND THE WORLD:

"Holy cr*p Patric! You packed more info into this killer little book than I've seen in $4,997 courses and seminars! I've seen first hand the difference it can make in people's lives when they take advantage of this kind of info. So, kudos to you for helping change lives, my friend."

Jason Oman, #1 International Best-Selling Author of Conversations with Millionaires

"Patric Chan blows you away with idea after idea for making money online. Keep a pen and paper handy as you read this book because the ideas ... and the cash ... will flow from the very first chapter."

Brett McFall, www.brettmcfall.com

"What a remarkable success story... Patric's techniques can be used by anyone with the will to win."

Jim Guarino, CEO

"Patric Chan used to answer my emails for me, but look at him now ... Through sheer persistence and an insatiable appetite for knowledge he has morphed into **one of the top Internet entrepreneurs on the planet.** This book alone is solid proof of that. I'd hire him back in a second, but this time I'd make him my VP of Marketing. Of course, he'd never accept because it would be a pay cut from the vast sums he's making now."

Mark Joyner, #1 Best-Selling Author of "Simpleology"

"Patric is one of the most enthusiastic and passionate people I know and he has had the GREAT sense to focus on what he does best, that focus has made him rich, and that focus is what so many people lack!

It will be a great honor for me and very smart to keep doing business with him as he has certainly helped my income. You would be wise to do the same! Well done and congratulations to this great man."

Marco Robinson, www.marcorobinson.com

"After completing your book, firstly let me say it was very easy to read and understand, I must say, I'm floored.

The main thoughts going through my head is "I just wish I had this information when I first started 10 years ago"! **I think if I had this information when "I" first started, I would be worth between 10 to 50 times what I'm worth right now.**

This is amazing information you are releasing, I've preordered a bunch of copies to give to my friends this Christmas.

Forgot to mention, the new twists you've put on your strategies, that I'd have never thought of in a million years. So I thank you, and my friends will also thank you.

Peter Drew, www.PeterDrew.net

"When I saw that Patric Chan shows people how to turn $10 into $1,000 through marketing smart online, I was skeptical. Although he backs that up with the real-world, simple -- and ingenious -- ways that anyone can follow to make their fortune."

Dan Klatt, Author

"Patric Chan is one of the most knowledgeable internet specialists today.

If there excited the "three internet musketeers" he would definitively be one of them, traveling the world teaching people about success using the power of the internet.

Come to think about it, that is exactly what he is doing now... By reading his latest book you will step into a world of knowledge that would normally take you years to achieve.

Fast track into the internet world by tapping into the brain and knowledge of Patric!

Receive the key information thousands of people normally have to go to a seminar to experience. Hep hep and away!"

Jarl Moe, International Speaker, www.jarlmoe.com

"Brutally honest, easy to read and understand for even the greenest newbie getting started. Patric covers a lot of ground, I'm quite amazed that he has fit so much into this one book. I wish I'd of had this myself back when I first started my online businesses. If you want to learn how to make money online, then this is highly recommended."

Jeremy Gislason, SureFireWealth, Inc. - SureFireWealth.com

"I like what Patric teaches because he's learned internet marketing from some of the best of the best and applied what he's learned to make great profits in his own business, and more importantly, he has learned how to teach others his system for generating income online. There are many valuable lessons and strategies and specific 'to-do's that Patric teaches that can (and should) be applied to create fast online profits.

Just one of the strategies that Patric mentions, I used my first two years in business to earn just over $185,000 in sales online. Patric knows what he's talking about and you'd be well-advised to take his instruction.

Patric's system is the right match for almost any new internet marketer, or you, the person who may have no experience online at all, but are looking for the fastest way to profits online. Let Patric be your teacher so you can gain from his insights and wisdom, and you too can build a successful online income stream (or streams)."

John W. Roney III

"It's wonderful that you've decided to share your invaluable experience and personal observations through this awesome book. The methods, techniques, ideas and tactics will help anyone with an online business or even just a website go from 'average' to A+.

"Best all of all, what you teach is 'simple' yet effective for any ordinary person to understand and use to his/her own advantage. "Well done.""

Mike Mograbi

1. WHAT CAN YOU DO WITH FIFTY BUCKS?

You can go out for a couple of coffees or beer. But I wouldn't suggest that because your body will be dehydrated.

Alternatively, you could start an online business with fifty bucks. I know it may sound ridiculous. To tell you the truth, I spent slightly more when I first set up my online business back in 2003.

Let me paint a clearer picture for you.

Imagine that you are running a business in the conventional world of selling products. You will have 2 main fixed costs -- the staff and office rental/mortgage. Then if your business revolves around selling, you definitely need staff for customer service and sales. Your other miscellaneous costs would be the electricity bill, water bill, phone bills, transportation, cleaners, etc. You can expect to fork out between $3,500 to $5,000 a month easily just for hiring 2 employees and renting a decent workable office.

Do remember that to set up a business in the offline or "brick and mortar" world, you will need to have your office renovated and decorated. Plus you will need to buy the office furniture and equipment like chairs, tables, phones, computers, software, cubicle partitions, etc. I am sure you will know that it is going to cost a bomb for someone who has a limited budget to get these. You could end up spending over $7,000 for a start. Hmm...

Now, let's examine the startup cost for an online business instead:

1. A computer. In this day and age who hasn't one or can't easily get one?

2. An internet connection. You are already paying the bill each month. Why not use it to create an income for yourself now?

1

3. A webpage creation software. You can get this free if you don't want to buy any advanced software. Let me just share this "secret" with you: it is called NVU, and you can download it for free at www.nvu.com.

4. Other additional software like audio recorder, image editor, documenting software, webmaster tools are all also available free, legally, if you know where to find them online.

Setup cost? $0.

Your fixed costs:

1. A domain name for your website. Dirt cheap. You can get it for $8.95 only, a year.

2. A host for your website. Less than $5 a month.

3. An automation system. You will need to have a kind of system to power your internet business such as email follow-ups, tracking software, affiliate management, etc. This has the same functionality as having a team of staff to manage and grow your business which will cost you approximately $3,000 in the offline world. Online? Dirt cheap again. Less than $50 a month. And get this--you can even avoid using any paid e-commerce system and simply rely on the free ones if you are on a shoestring budget!

So here is how much your monthly costs are for building a conventional business and an online one:

A.   Conventional offline business: $3,500 to $5,000 a month with an initial setup of approximately $7,000.

B.   Online business: less than $55 a month. In fact, if you don't want to use a more sophisticated automation system, you can have an online business set up and running profitably for less than $10! Ten dollars a month. That is less than 35 cents a day!

If you were wondering why you would want to pay for certain systems or software when you can get them for free, it is this: the paid ones are usually more user-friendly, advertisement free, better quality and can complete your tasks more quickly. You can always invest in them later on when you are making some nice cash. So don't worry, just use the free ones first to get your business going. (By the way, when I say "free software" I don't mean pirated software! I do mean legitimate free programs -- there are plenty of them online.)

When you think about it, the cost of entry to start an online business is insanely low. The day I started making money online, I could never consider setting up conventional businesses again. For a small cost, I could get the yield return of 10,000 per cent! I could turn $10 to $1,000 or more. If you are not jumping on this money-making bandwagon today, you are losing out on one of the biggest opportunities that ever existed in our time.

One more thing that is worth mentioning: ten bucks is just like having a cup of coffee and a piece of cake at a cafe. Can you skip those and invest in your future instead?

Here is a "crash course" guideline to start an online business:

Research for a profitable niche market and create or obtain a product to sell in it. Once you have found this demand, set up your website as your storefront or else no one can buy from you. At the same time, make sure you have a simple system to build your subscriber or customer database for future sales follow up. Once these are all taken care of, start to drive traffic (i.e. people browsing online) to your webpage and convert them into leads and customers.

From there, continue to grow your business by applying new methods or enhance the techniques you are using with success for better results.

Simple yet effective.

Now let's look closer at the costs:

1. Find your market. Free, except for your time.

2. Set up your webpage and write the sales letter. Again free except for your time and some "brain-work". The domain name would probably cost you $8.95 per year from godaddy.com and $5 a month for the hosting.

3. Create or obtain a product to sell. Cost = $0.

4. Collecting payment online. There are several companies on the internet that provide this type of service but you can always use the free ones. The most famous one would be Paypal.com. Cost to register? $0.

5. A simple system to build your database and email follow-up software. The free ones normally have ads or limited features but you can definitely get a free service to use temporarily.

6. Driving traffic. There are tons of methods that you can use for free and yet are effective. One of the best free ones I use is getting joint venture partners for promotions. Works like a charm. And it works in any type of niche market.

So if you are still mulling over getting started in business because you think that you have limited funds, guess what? You just need $50 to get started! Isn't that good news?

Come to think of it, you will be investing by using your credit card anyway. That being the case, you are literally starting a business with "no money down". You then get 30 solid days to make some cash to pay back your credit card company ... like a measly 50 dollars? Worst case-- even if you failed, you just lose a couple of drinks with that amount of money.

2. BUILDING YOUR ONLINE BUSINESS WITH EMAIL MARKETING

Email marketing is one of the most effective marketing methods nowadays simply because virtually almost everyone uses email. In my opinion, a person without an email address will be considered weird for this generation. At the same time, email marketing campaigns carried out improperly can offend a lot of people.

The not-so-secret way to surmount this dilemma is through permission-based email marketing. It is stupid to send email to all the people and then get nasty replies. Just send to those who have shown interest in what you have to tell. The key to this predicament is to have a very discerning eye about who to email and who to not email. Better look for some metrics on how to know which group of people would give you high ROI, or return on investment.

The Real Deal With Building Opt-in Lists

Building an opt-in list isn't easy, particularly for newbies. However, knowing your subscribers' interest will help you lower your expenses and create more sales.

Devise a tactic to make people voluntarily provide you with the information necessary to create higher conversion. The most basic information you need to start an email marketing campaign is the First Name and Email address. The extras like phone number, last name, mailing address, etc. are useful but not necessary.

Ask only for their first name and email address in opt-ins. Make sure that the profiles you gather are updated to aid in improving the relevance and satisfaction from each deal you make.

An old adage says it all -- "action speaks louder than words". This easily translates to the difficulty one has to undergo during the execution of his or her email marketing efforts. It is not just about sending emails. If they are not structured carefully, they can leave a very bad impression on your subscribers.

Tracking your email marketing results can also be tough. Technology and relevant sources should be employed in making this aspect of your marketing a lot more manageable. The reason you want to track is so that you know how many clicks you are getting and what are the conversion rates.

Don't Make Your Point Of Sale Pointless

Each time you sell something, make sure you collect the customers' email address. These are the most responsive mailing lists you can ever have.

Profit Later, Build Your List First

The easiest way to get someone to subscribe to your mailing list is to offer a "bribe". Give a valuable free gift in exchange for their name and email address. I am not asking you to give away stupid gifts. If you want to offer a gift, do it right in the first place. Make sure you are giving a useful and valuable gift for free or else it will backfire because the content of your free gift will reflect how deep is your knowledge of the given niche market you are in.

Surprisingly -- Not!

Having a website is never a guarantee that your online business will succeed. How can you succeed if people don't realize that your business exists online? The key to internet marketing is to get your business noticed by having the ability to reach your prospective customers at any time you want, which is by using email.

Decide On Your Niche Market Or Target Market

It is absolutely essential to know your target market in order to focus on something. It is really confusing and time consuming if you build an opt-in list with no particular market in mind. You would not know what offers to present to your subscribers. For instance, it is silly to send golf-related offers to a list of subscribers who are interested in flower arranging.

Moreover, having a niche market would bring more focus to your marketing campaigns and would derive better results because you have directed your emails to people who would most likely be interested in them.

Verify If Your Chosen Target Market Is An Income Generating Market

Building a highly targeted opt-in list will just go to waste if your subscribers are not generating any income at all.

No orders = No money

Try to verify their income generating potential through the search engines. You will find some paid ads related to the keywords you have searched for in Google.com. This means that if somebody is willing to pay to advertise focusing on the same target market that you have in mind, chances are, you will be able to reap positive results on your target market. So, no, your product or target market does not need to be "the only one out there" or "the first in the world"!

The main purpose of your email marketing is to reach your target audience as quickly and as directly as possible. You need to reach your target market to promote products and services that would benefit your target customers. (Most businesses use email marketing to only maintain contact and relationship with their customers.) The reason why email marketing has grown at such an unprecedented rate is because people in the virtual community are always hungry for information. They subscribe to information that they are interested in. Besides, email is still free to use, at the time of this writing.

On the other hand, not everyone is willing to subscribe to such information. They may be interested in your products once but may no longer be interested to buy again. Moreover, when you continue to send emails without their permission, you can be accused of spamming.

When you build an opt-in list, you not only increase the probability of being successful in email marketing but also boost your sales and profits as well. This is because building such a list will give you the chance to stay in contact with your customers by getting their (most current and probably most active) email addresses. But *this statement is only applicable if you know how to write and send emails that can generate cash for you.*

In this manner, you can continue to promote your products and services which they are interested in because they have opted to subscribe to your mailing list. Hence, whatever it is that you feed them, chances are, they will most   likely   respond   positively.

Writing Your Emails

The first thing to consider before getting your email read is to get your reader's attention to read it! I know this statement sounds "twisted" but if you read it carefully again, you will understand what I mean.

Write Your Emails As Personal As Possible

One of the most powerful personal email writing strategies is "The Personal Story Opening".

This opening simply means that you include some personal note about yourself in the opening sentence with the objective being that everyone likes to do business with a "real" person.

For example, in one of these messages I stated in the opening,

"What a week ... my computer monitor blew out and my printer is spitting out garbage ... "

Here are a few more examples of this type of opening:

"Before I got involved in internet marketing, I was selling and organizing self-improvement seminars. I started in 2003 ... and in my mind, online business is a nearly 'perfect' business!"

If you are on my email list, you will notice the personal touch attached to most of my emails. They are short... but more importantly, they remind my subscribers that there is a "real person" behind the messages they are getting. Sometimes I talk about my hobby or something else about my personal life that is brief and not too revealing. It adds a touch of warmth, which some subscribers need to make them more receptive to my messages.

The key to the success of this opening is to make it brief; one short sentence is all you need.

* Note: Find out my recommended autoresponder at www.sendaweber.com

3. TWO WAYS TO CREATE A PROFITABLE INFO-PRODUCT

There are 2 types of approaches you can choose from when it comes to creating an info product. It is either you be creative or be innovative.

Being *creative* means you observe the market and come up with a good solution. Basically, it is using your own brain to think of how your info product can solve the existing problems of your prospective customers. For instance, you see a lot of people having a problem writing sales letters and you come up with a sales letter generator software. Or you notice many people trying to organize their joint venture's details and you create a joint venture profile software.

Anyway, being *creative* basically means you are the first person to hit the market with your unique product.

However, if you want to minimize the risk of failure and make money fast, you should be an *innovator*! An innovator observes the existing products created to fulfil the demands of a market, sees how good the sales volume is, and then provides a better solution to tap into the existing opportunity.

Not sure what this means? Let me explain with some real life situations.

An example of an *innovator* marketer is a company by the name of JVZoo which provides a service similar to Clickbank.com. Clickbank.com was the first (that I know of) website to provide credit card processing service with a built-in affiliate tracking program for internet marketers to use.

Today there are many other innovative marketers that have created affiliate tracking tools which can be integrated with other credit card processors, e.g. Paypal.com and Stripe.

Innovative marketing is not limited to copying what is successful and trying to be better, bigger or cheaper. That is a very narrow understanding on how to be profitable and such products normally fail.

So how should we do it? Well, just by adding these 2 extra ingredients -- and you will change the whole profit model:

#1| Finding An Angle

This means finding a way to position yourself uniquely from the originator. Example, Clickbank.com was a success. Credit card processing companies normally don't come with a built-in affiliate tracking system for merchants, but Clickbank.com has this feature--for free use. It solves the core problem of online merchants.

#2| Complementing The Pioneer

Create an info product that can ride on the existing successful market. Let's take Clickbank.com again as our example. Many new tools have been created by innovators to enhance the convenience of using Clickbank. These include software to manage your Clickbank.com affiliates, software to research for Clickbank top sellers, video tutorials about Clickbank marketing, etc.

Observe what is happening on the *internet. Then decide whether to become either a creative or an* innovative marketer. It will give you more profit but reduce your work load. Then, *take action.*

4. WHAT I LEARNED AT THE WORLD INTERNET SUMMIT

I discovered 3 valuable internet marketing tips at the World Internet Summit seminar when I spoke there, more than 10 years ago...

#1 | Ask The Right Questions

If you are not getting the answers to your problems, it could because you are not asking the right questions. I have noticed many people asking general questions like:

o "How do I get traffic to my website?"
o "How do I make money online?"
o "How do I write an ebook?"

If you ask general questions, you will get general answers -- simple as that. For instance, if someone asked me how to make money online, I will tell him or her to sell info products. But will that answer solve the problem? Yes, but it hardly gives any real solution.

#2 | Create As Many Small Niche Online Businesses As Possible

When Brett McFall was showing his presentation, he showed one of his niche sites that was making an average income of US$1,000 plus a month---on autopilot!

If you think US$1,000 plus a month is nothing to shout about, you are right... but imagine if you could have 10 of these sites running for you on autopilot, you will be making US$10,000 plus every month!

Start small and once you get the momentum rolling, it will be easy for you to grow your income. If you can imagine that earning one million dollars a year from the internet is fun and exciting, think of how you are going to make a thousand a month first. Once you have learnt the "tricks", you can easily build more internet businesses that will create multiple online income streams.

#3| You Need A Team To Run A Multi-Million-Dollar Internet Business

After the seminar in Shanghai, Tom Hua, the co-founder of World Internet Summit took us to visit his software development office. One thing for sure -- he has an awesome office... and plenty of staff managing his multi-million-dollar internet business.

Then, I asked other speakers and a few of them actually have a team and an office as well. It does not matter whether you have staff or partners, but you do need a team if you want to grow your online business to its full potential.

Let's say your internet business is to create new courses and sell it on the internet. Ideally, you should have a team of people to help you do research and designs (of the webpages and products), handle customer service once it's launched and so on. Remember, a team does not necessarily mean that your people are on a fixed salary; they could be engaged on a project basis. The point is, you have a group of talented people who are available to help you when you need them.

So it's a good idea to start building a team right now. You will be prepared by then.

5. A REAL SECRET ABOUT ACHIEVING SUCCESS ON THE INTERNET?

Isn't it great to finally understand that nothing is holding you back from succeeding online except taking action? The bottom line: If you are persistent and take action on a daily basis you can have success in your life.

Not convinced yet? Ok, let's plod on because you will be.

All you have to do is be persistent about working toward what you want and BINGO! You will get there!

Isn't that great news? You don't have to be special or rich or have an advanced degree--you just need to be persistent!

There is one thing you need to do to keep yourself motivated toward success--at least it helps me and I know it works: *Real students of success love to read about successful people in their chosen field.*

Why?

It's because you can "learn" from them, see what other successful people have done, how they overcame obstacles, setbacks and disappointments. You can overcome anything once you know how by using the right role models. For example, great students of "creating wealth from businesses" love to read biographies of successful entrepreneurs.

If the idea of spending a whole week to read a book turns you off, then think of it as a learning experience. If you still hate it, then you probably should consider a field other than "starting businesses". There is no shame in saying you are just not cut out for it. Move on and do what you really love.

You have a choice to find another business to be in. I love marketing and self-improvement, be it online or offline. It is the most exciting business I can ever hope to be involved in. But if I ever stopped learning, I am dead. You have to be a "student" in business if you are going to succeed online or offline.

Persistence is important to be successful. With persistence and continual learning, ordinary people can be successful. It doesn't take super-smart people to achieve that.

6. WHY PEOPLE JUST CAN'T MAKE IT

You can easily "write" an ebook and start selling it online (or maybe put it on Amazon Kindle)... even if you're not an expert on that topic.

If you're not knowledgeable...

It's a relatively easy process, the method is simple - pick up 5-6 books about that particular topic and read all of them. By the time you've completed reading, you would probably know a little bit of that topic. Then come up with your own words and summaries of what you've learned and the next thing you know, you'll have a "book" in you.

Don't get me wrong – I'm not suggesting you to copy in any way. That's unethical and totally uncool.

I mean, if you read a book about persuasion techniques, you'll find almost the same content in another persuasion technique book.

Same thing with parenting and relationship information - most of the advice is the same but it's just being explained (or taught) differently.

Of course, there will be times when you'll discover novel content about persuasion or relationships or parenting in a book but my point here is, you can create your own information product easily with some basic research.

And everybody knows that having your own information product is the ULTIMATE key for long term internet marketing success. I mean, just look at a dude who sells a course about how to make money from Facebook - isn't the WAY how he's making money is none other than selling HIS information product to you? I rest my case.

What's wrong with most people who are trying to make long term money online is they know how to make money online (which is to create and sell their own information products) but they are not doing that because product creation is a lot of work.

Do you know what I think is the most important skill of internet marketing that can literally guarantee you to make money?

Be really good at copywriting. Heck, if you can do that, you don't even need traffic.

Why? Well, if you can increase conversion (assuming you're a really good copywriter), you can just approach any guy or gal online who has an existing product with traffic and say...

"Let me increase the sales conversion of your sales letter and for any new sales increment, we'll split 50/50."

Or you can write for marketers and get paid handsomely.

The problem? To become a GOOD copywriter requires a lot of hard work and it doesn't happens overnight.

So people try to find shortcuts - they try to figure out how to make money from "hot trends", looking for a "better" software to buy, searching for Facebook loopholes and the list goes on. That's perfect but don't expect these to give you a BUSINESS. They're just short term opportunities.

What is the message of my rant here?

You can never go wrong on making money online by creating your own information product and learning how to write good copy (or record a video) that gets people wanting to buy. THESE ARE THE 2 THINGS YOU NEED TO MASTER.

What about traffic? Well, if you have a product and know it'll convert, just use money to buy traffic!

Last but not least, don't get my message wrongly - do continue to try to make money from Facebook or review sites and so on because they can be lucrative but make sure that you're ALSO taking care of your future by creating your own information product.

7. CAN'T FIND "NEW" INFORMATION?

Do me a favor. Go to the shelf, look at your books (or ebooks) and pick up the book that you think provides the most information for you. Or go and buy that ebook you saw a few days ago that you think will give you lots of new ideas or catapult you to success.

Guess what? You might end up disappointed because you are not going to find a book that has all the latest or newest information. (If you're a personal improvement fella, you'll know what I mean. Your bookshelf would probably have several books on the same topic related to achieving success in life.)

Let's say you have read 15 ebooks on how to generate traffic to your website. Then you find a new ebook that claims to reveal 10 "new" traffic generation strategies and you buy it. To be honest, you might learn only one or two new strategies from it. Most of the other strategies are those which you have already heard of or been exposed to.

But guess what? I would be happy to learn just one new traffic generation idea from that book! And it doesn't end there. I would be delighted to read about the other 9 strategies that I already know!

Why? Because this gives me more assurance that the other 9 strategies do work--otherwise, all those other people won't be claiming how useful it is!

Yet it doesn't end there. Here's why. Each time I read an ebook teaching about traffic generation, I find that most internet gurus say that writing articles will bring more traffic. Each time I read that, I will take action immediately and start writing a new article.

See what happens? Each time I read, I take action. Each time I take action, I get results. So if I hadn't read that book that gave me repeated information, I would never have thought of writing a new article.

What's the lesson? Don't just go trying to find new ideas, but look at old ideas as a reminder of your present situation.

Does it end here? Nope. There are advantages to reading an ebook in which the content is repeated information. Let me tell you what happened to me one time. As I was browsing through the content of an internet marketing membership, I came to an article titled, "Underground Traffic". Curious like a cat, I wanted to know what this "underground" thing was. So I started to read.

And I found out this underground traffic tactic is to use expired domains to get their existing traffic when the owners did not renew their domain names.

At first, I thought, "That's an `old' strategy. I've heard of it before."

Then it came to me -- "Wait a minute... if I've heard of it, why haven't I used it?"

See what happened here? If I had not read about the underground traffic tactic again, I would never have used this strategy in my business--ever!

And finally, "repeat" information may lead you to more new ideas. Of course, you will need to be a little bit more creative here. But that should not be a problem because as you learn more tactics over the years, "mixing and matching" them becomes easier. You will have many "Eureka!" moments if you keep learning "new" and relearning "old" stuff.

For instance, if buying expired domains can bring traffic, what other ideas can you come up with to make more money online? How about, selling off that domain again for a higher price when there is consistent traffic coming to it?

So don't go around complaining about getting the same information when you read a book or purchase a new one. It all depends on how you want to benefit from it. If you go looking for chinks in a shining armor, guess what will you find? Even the tiniest hole that only an ant can fit into will justify your logic.

8. CREATE YOUR FIRST NICHE MARKETING PRODUCT

Let's say you decide to create a "how-to" product that teaches people to cook. You can surely go to the library or bookstore and get some ideas on layout, table of contents, etc.

Do you know what? A how-to manual is just a bunch of reports/articles put together in a logical sequence. Do your research, look at other books and reports, and start putting your articles together. Remember this, it doesn't have to be hundreds of pages to make you money. If the reader finds it useful, he/she will be willing to pay you for it.

The great thing about short informational products (delivered via the internet) is that you can make a profit even if you sell it for a few bucks. Most of my products are less than 20 pages in length, and sell for between US$9.95 and US$39.95.

More money is being made out there than ever before, by individuals selling short, focused reports! And it is growing at incredible rates. The bottom line is, when it comes to info products, size doesn't necessarily matter! *Quality does!*

You could make just as much money with a 15 page book as you can with a 100 page work. In fact, you can make more with the shorter book. I will show you how shortly.

Profit potential aside, there are many other great reasons to create these little ebooks, for instance:

o They are very easy to put together; they don't require much work;
o They can be completed within a few weeks, a few days, and sometimes even a few hours;

o They are really not that difficult or time consuming to market;

o They are especially great for new marketers (with little or no experience) and are also easy profit generators for seasoned marketers; and ...

o Most importantly, they allow you to spread your risk.

You see, it all boils down to time and money, i.e. time management and positive cash flow.

Time is a very precious commodity, especially if you still have a 9 to 5 job to deal with. And we already know that all of our projects will not be home runs. In fact, there is a good chance that a few of them will be complete flops. That's the reality most of us have to deal with.

So, if you invest a lot of time and energy into creating a monster ebook that turns out to be a dud, a total failure, you would have lost all the time and the energy you put into that project, with nothing to show for it.

On the other hand, if you had spent only a couple of weeks to create a much shorter ebook which also turned out to be a dud, you could quickly pull that one out and replace it with another short one. Your risks are dramatically reduced and your chances of putting out a winner are increased!

It is better to create 10 little ebooks per year and have 2 of them strike out -- which means 8 of them are bringing in the cash! Better than to only create one or two big ebooks in that same year and risk having both of them flop with nothing to show for your efforts that year. There is also a much better chance that one of your products will be a hot seller if you have 10 of them out there, instead of just one or two.

Now, let's look at profit potential. If each one of these 8 books brings in US$1,000 per month for you, the profits can add up quickly. If your goal is to pull in US$100,000 in the coming year, you have a much better chance of getting there with 8 to 10 small ebooks bringing in $1,000 per month each, instead of relying on just one big ebook alone to pull in the entire US$100,000. Makes sense, doesn't it?

And even if you earn just a few hundred dollars per month from each of the 8 books, that is still a heck of a lot better than what most people are making online!

Here are a few more ways you can ensure that you profit from these short ebooks well into the future:

o You can offer each one as a backend (follow-up) product for the other.

o You can bundle them up later and sell them as a brand new package, with a different price tag.

o You can use some of them (especially if they don't sell too well on their own) as bonuses for your other products, to increase the perceived value of the package.

o You can also use some of them purely as list builders. For example, give them away for free, swap them with other marketers, or do whatever with them as long as you get more mileage. The fact that it only took you a week or two to create them offers you a lot more options and flexibility.

But if you are still passionate about creating that monster ebook, why not break it up into smaller projects and start selling each one as they get completed?

For example, if you want to create the "complete" cook book, you could start by creating a small ebook on just low carbs recipes and start selling it. Then, create another on "sweet desserts" and get that one out as well. And so on...

In the end, you can bundle them up together, or combine them into one mega book and sell it. Your time is much better spent that way. And you also have some cash coming in while you work on your projects.

Many of us continue to chase after that single million dollar idea and miss many of the smaller hundred thousand dollar projects along the way.

These smaller products are much easier to create, are much easier to roll out, don't require a large investment of your time, energy or money, and they greatly reduce your risks.

They are also probably the fastest way to get your name out there and build credibility for yourself and your business. You can really do some serious "damage" with these mini ebooks, as long as you provide valuable information in them.

After your product is done, convert your manuscript to PDF so that it caters to both PC and Mac users.

Nevertheless, one of the biggest questions that people want to know is how to protect your PDF ebooks from being distributed illegally to others.

There are applications out there that can prevent this problem by 'locking' the PDF file into an "exe" file so that it will require a password or license code to access it.

And of course, you can always take legal action to the distributor locally or internationally. However, normally I don't do that (unless the wrongdoer is based locally then it is easier to take legal action) because *I want to spend* my time to *sell more copies than thinking about how to "save" the sales*. We have to think about reaching the masses with the internet and because the reach is so wide, sometimes, it doesn't matter much if our work is being distributed illegally by a few individuals.

Let me explain it this way: John in Chicago bought your ebook. John loves it and he sends it to his friend, Robert in Alabama. Now, Robert may not even know that you exist so even if John had not sent it to Robert, you would most likely never be able to reach Robert anyway. But since John did, he has helped you to spread your brand across the state--and Robert may end up being a future customer of yours! So you need to think bigger and broader, friends.

This is why I don't focus too much effort on protecting my ebooks over the internet internationally. But if they are being pirated locally, I will take action because such illegal distribution will affect my bottom line.

Now, let's start cranking out your first ebook or report to sell today!

9. FORGET ABOUT BIG SUCCESS

Some time ago, I've shared some valuable tips on how to make money online in our live seminar called, Multiple Streams of Income In A Flash. These include the technique on how to make $100K a year by working just a day a month, how to make money with flippa.com and the secret on how to build a mailing list with newsletter advertising.

We have over 200 attendees – ranging from newbies to experienced marketers who are already making money online. Some of the questions I've gotten were:

How do I get rank in Google on page #1?

How do I get a lot of paid members for my monthly membership?

How do I get Joint Venture Partners to promote my product now?

How do I get instant traffic?

Here are the answers:

"How do I get rank in Google on page #1?"

You spend a lot of time on keyword research, build a search-engine friendly website with keyword optimized content and get backlinks like crazy every day. Continue to do that diligently and the 'magic' can happen.

"How do I get a lot of paid members to my monthly membership?"

Start building your mailing list first, right now. Then convert your mailing list to paid members by over-delivering your content.

"How do I get Joint Venture Partners to promote my product now?"

Build a relationship first, only then send your JV proposal and make sure that your proposal is very attractive.

"How do I get instant traffic?"

Well, buy traffic with Google Adwords or paid advertising from other's newsletters.

Which of course, these aren't the answers that people want to hear (although those are the RIGHT solutions) – simply because, the truth is, it costs MONEY OR TIME to make internet marketing work.

What people did not realize is… these solutions are ALREADY saving you money and time.

If there's another 'secret' to internet marketing secret, then it's this:

Small success is better than no success.

You see, many people are still living in their dreams that ONE DAY, one fine day; they are going to make a million from the internet magically. Could be that they wrote a super amazing ebook that sells for $20 and sold 50,000 copies or founded another Twitter or something. Could happen, who knows.

The problem is, they want this BIG success but haven't even mastered the basic stuff yet.

This is like saying, I want to be Michael Jordan (during his basketball peak days) but I still don't know how to play basketball yet. For those who know Michael Jordan's bio, they'll know that Michael started with 'small' success before he became extremely good. So did Bruce Lee. Or Robert Kiyosaki with his Rich Dad, Poor Dad best-seller hit. Heck, so does EVERYONE, including internet marketers.

Because there are so many stories of how ordinary people strike fortunes online, people started to think that the Internet is an ATM machine. On top of that, all of those hype courses just add more fuel to this dream.

As weird as it sounds, at the same time, the Internet IS a form of an ATM machine. Like, if you build a list and add value to it all of the time, well, it's a form of ATM machine, isn't it?

But where does the money from the ATM machine comes from? It's the money you've put in (or the interest you've gotten from your money). The point is, you got to work to put the money in it.

Start by putting in a little. You'll wake up one day, astonished at what you've accomplished after a period of time.

If you haven't read the book WakeUp Millionaire, this is exactly what I mean. Just go to Amazon.com and search for "WakeUp Millionaire" and get yourself a copy. It's less than $10.

10. HOW TO WRITE POWERFUL JOINT VENTURE PROPOSALS

Did you know that many joint venture offers end up in the "Trash" folder, not because of poor products but because of poor joint venture proposals?

Joint ventures (JV) have been proven to be one of the most effective methods to gain business quickly and easily. In a nutshell, JVs are powerful because they enable you to leverage on other people's time, money, effort and anything else.

However there is a problem--the problem of writing a powerful JV proposal to get your potential partner to say "Yes" to your offer.

Here are 5 important pointers you should have if you want your proposal to be more powerful and effective:

#1| Give More Than Normal

Don't think about yourself. Give your potential JV partner the advantage of gaining more benefits from you. If you are offering commission, give more than 50 per cent commission. If you are building a database, give him the possibility to gain more than you.

Don't just think win-win; think how they can win *much more than you.*

#2| Do You Have Any Perks?

Let's say, you are trying to "recruit" a potential partner to join a paid program like an online multilevel marketing so that he can endorse it to his list as well. What perks can you offer him? How do you differentiate yourself from several other members of the same program?

An example of a perk you can do is to pay for him the membership site's fee for the first month so that he can try it out. If he gets hooked and endorses it, you will get many times the return. If not, all you lose is the fee of a month's membership.

#3 | Make Them Like You

Even if you have a super valuable product but your potential JV partners don't like you, they probably won't accept your offer. Why? Because there are thousands of products similar to yours that they can sell! So your product is not really exclusive in that respect.

But how do you make them like you?

If you can, buy their products. Normally, everyone treats their customers as special. If you have become their customer, I believe you will get special treatment or personal attention. If you cannot afford their products, at least subscribe to their newsletter.

#4 | Short And Sweet

Don't write a long JV proposal. I personally delete those long letters without reading them. You must understand and respect your potential JV partner's time. You must always assume they are very busy people. Get to the point. Write a short, specific and "sweet" proposal.

#5 | Gain Credibility First

If possible, quote some other names familiar to your potential JV partner showing that they have accepted your proposal. The reason is, not many people like to be the first person to promote your product if it is a new one without a proven track record. If someone has tried it with success, this will lower their risk of things backfiring on them for promoting your product.

Use these five ingredients and I am convinced that your JV proposals will get more "yes" responses from today onwards.

11. DO EBOOKS SELL?

Despite what you may have been told, the answer is and always will be "yes". People have and always will be prepared to pay for information in ebook format.

You see, one of the strongest human desires is to learn, to be educated and to better ourselves, no matter what the subject is. It could be to live longer and healthier, to be a better parent, partner or lover, to raise children well, to earn more money, to work fewer hours, to own a nicer home or a faster car, to be better at sports, or to bake tastier cakes--everyone wants to learn! People want information and nearly all are prepared to pay for it.

Ebooks have become desirable because of their instant nature. Once ordered, all the information needed is downloaded into that person's computer. No hassle, no waiting, no fuss. Instant gratification.

Have you bought an ebook online before? If yes, that's the proof it works.

As an "info publisher" you can earn a substantial income and put in far fewer hours than the average person working the 9 to 5 treadmill by selling ebooks. You can fit in work time when it is convenient and from the comfort of your own home.

Alternatively you can put the knowledge here to work for only a couple of hours each week and you can still make a healthy second income (if you want to keep your job). How hard you work and how much you make is up to you. But nothing comes for free. *YOU MUST BE PREPARED TO LEARN AND THEN TO PUT IT INTO PRACTICE. IF YOU DO YOU WILL BE SUCCESSFUL; IF YOU DON'T YOU WILL FAIL.*

I cannot express this strongly enough. You would be amazed at just how many people fail by default ... simply because they never took action.

What Type Of eBook Will People Buy?

The answer is simple: almost any type as long as it offers a solution to a "problem". There are thousands of people interested in thousands of topics. The secret is: Discover a need, target the market and feed it.

What Is Your eBook's USP?

An ebook's unique selling proposition (USP) is a single, unique benefit that makes your ebook stand out from those of your competitors. Even before you start to key in any words to your ebook, you must establish what it is.

Your ebook's USP should influence everything you write. It should be the one unique strength or advantage that you and only you can deliver because there are tons of other ebooks having the same topic as yours.

All the best to your ebook business!

12. GETTING STATS TO RESEARCH A NICHE?

Most people will determine an online niche market to be profitable or not based on keyword tools like the Google Keyword Tool. They will then find the number of searches a month for certain keywords from search engines like Google, Yahoo, MSN, etc. And most marketers will tell you a certain yardstick number of searches will be good to determine how profitable that niche can be.

If you are still using this strategy -- *oh, boy*!

First of all, this strategy is correct. It makes sense. The problem with it is you are not applying any marketing techniques in it. You are relying on how profitable a niche can be based on reported numbers only!

Besides, this is an "old" technique. I think the first time I heard about this strategy was way back a couple of years ago. Does it still work? Yes -- but you are missing out on so many other ways to determine how profitable a niche can be.

I mean, let's say the keyword "lobster" has 30,000++ searches. Based on the number, it is a good sign. But really, do you think you can make money in this "lobster" niche?

Maybe, maybe not. But for me, I will definitely make sure that I have researched it by using the numbers and marketing strategies first.

The next question is what is the medium that you are going to use to make money in this niche? Sell lobsters online? I doubt it. So really, numbers don't tell. The worst is when you are not applying any marketing concepts and senses to it.

Let me share with you a "filter" method that I teach my students...

Finding Hardcore Believers/Followers

There are certain niche markets that have people willing to spend. These are the "believers" or "followers". It is really hard for me to tell you which niches these are, but as a simple guideline, ask yourself, "How much do they really need it?"

For instance, model train hobbyists are crazy spenders for anything related to "model trains".

If your niche is "save marriage", you will have a very profitable online niche market because these people need the information desperately. The value of getting the problem solved is worth many times the cost of your product.

Building a successful online business is no guessing game. It is a matter of making no money, some money, or *a lot of money*! It can be scientifically "predicted" to ensure your risk of failing will be very low.

You need to have an overall marketing system to build a long-term profitable online business, and getting into the *right* niche is one element you cannot dismiss.

13. HOW TO GET FREE TRAFFIC BY GIVING AWAY A FREE EBOOK

This may come as a surprise. Or not. It depends on how much knowledge and experience you have with internet marketing.

I am sharing this tip with you because I have proof of its success. This strategy has been used for ages by internet marketers. The strategy is to offer freebies, especially a free eBook, to get traffic to your site. I have been enjoying a healthy amount of traffic each day with this strategy for years.

Here is an idea I use. I have another webpage that focuses on self-improvement topics at www.youchanbewealthy.com. Feel free to subscribe to that, too, if you have a desire to improve your life through self-improvement.

Okay. Let's get back to our strategy. I offer a free eBook from the webpage. To date, I have received thousands of downloads for the eBook and generated traffic to www.youchanbewealthy.com from the link in it.

The strange thing is, there are so many people using this strategy but have failed to achieve any successful results. Why?

Here are 5 tips to help you achieve successful "viral marketing" by offering a free eBook:

#1| Your eBook Must Be Valuable

Here is a rule of thumb. Your eBook *must* have value to the readers. That means there must be something they can learn or gain from it. Common sense will tell you, if the book is full of garbage, what makes them want to share it with their friends?

Preferably, before you give away the book, think of this first: If you sell it for any price, will there be a buyer? If your answer is yes, you have a winner.

#2 | It Must Not Be Boring

Imagine this. It is free. Most likely, it will not be appreciated as much as a paid book. So, the way you write the eBook and compile it *must* have a "flow" that makes it interesting to read--or it will end up in the recycle bin!

#3 | Get Other People To Help By Distributing It

If you want it to spread fast, you need other marketers with big lists to help you promote your free eBook. If you do it by yourself, it is going to take a very long time to spread it unless you are like #1 in search engine ranking. The best way to get it distributed is to find marketers who have existing subscribers is to share your free eBook.

#4 | There Should Not Be Too Many Affiliate Links

Provide only links that portray sincerity in your part on giving your readers convenience to find more information or resources. So don't promote everything under the sun. Too many affiliate links will turn off any reader as it will look obvious that you are trying to earn backend sales from affiliate programs. Nobody likes to be sold to, not even you, correct?

#5 | Make Your Book "Brandable"

I don't think the word "brandable" is in the dictionary. But brandable to my understanding means that the readers can brand your eBook with their own name, url or affiliate link (in that eBook). This tip is the most important! If you download my above mentioned eBook, you will see that I offer my readers the ability to brand it with their own link. It just makes sense, doesn't it?

People will like to give away your eBook if they can also get free traffic or backend sales. This is also one of the main reasons why my viral marketing strategy has been so successful thus far.

Let me give you an example. In the past, I have contacted promotion partners to give away my $27 eBook called, You *"Chan" Be Wealthy* for free. In this eBook, there are links to product, the WakeUp Millionaire.

That eBook was "branded" with their own names, website urls and their affiliate link to my product to earn sales commission. So when their readers end up buying it from the link recommended inside, my promotion partners got paid

50 per cent commission!

So if your free eBook is not brandable, then there is no incentive to attract promotion partners to give it to their readers even when it's free. Right now with the branded copy, not only they are adding great value to their readers by giving a $27 eBook for free, they are also promoting their own websites (which are listed in your eBook) and enjoying the possibility of generating affiliate commission.

You might already be giving away a free eBook at this moment. But apply the above 5 tips, and your eBook will spread like wildfire. And if you don't have a free eBook to give away yet, what are you waiting for?

14. HOW ARE YOU GOING TO MAKE MONEY ONLINE THIS YEAR?

There are only 2 ways for you to make money online. Either you sell your own product or you sell other people's products as an affiliate. Don't limit yourself to one income stream -- do both.

It is important to create your own product if you want to make money online. Back in 2004, I authored the eBook, *How To Make More Money Easily*, and created the *5-Step System To Make Money Online* DVD package, for the simple reason that, if you have your own product, you can be a better affiliate marketer by offering your own product as a gift to those who purchased through your affiliate link.

(Note: Both are no longer available – they're discontinued courses because I've already developed the latest courses to replace them.)

Secondly, if you have an awesome product and everyone is dying to have a copy of it, you will be able to create your own affiliate program and leverage on other people's efforts to get sales.

If you are thinking, "Nobody will buy the product that I create," don't worry. You can create a product to sell other people's products instead of selling the product you created. Confused?

For example, if you want to sell an autoresponder software, you can write a short eBook like *20 Hidden Ways To Increase Sales By Using Autoresponder Emails*. Then give this eBook away for free. In it, recommend the autoresponder you want to promote as an affiliate, like www.sendaweber.com.

This eBook will act as the content provider, i.e. telling the readers how they can increase their sales by using an autoresponder software but ultimately, they will need the software to apply the strategy taught. But notice this, you have essentially created a product.

Here's an extra tip to maximize the potential of creating your own free product. Pick a product that you want to promote that has a 2-tier commission structure in which the merchant pays out commission to you if you sell his product. At the same time, if you "recruited" affiliates for them, they will pay you a 2-tier commission for whatever sales are generated by your recruited affiliates.

Now you understand how 2-tier works, your next step is to recruit other affiliates. Instead of approaching them to make a direct promotion for the merchant (owner of the affiliate program), tell them that they can give away your product for free and customize it with their affiliate links. Once they have promoted your free product on their website or to their subscribers, you will earn 2-tier affiliate commission for their work.

With this simple method, you will be able to leverage on others by creating your own product.

15. AN EASY WAY TO INCREASE SALES INSTANTLY

Most internet marketers constantly think about how to generate more website traffic or how to increase the size of their list. Although that is the obvious way to increase sales and make more money online, let me teach you a better way. It is called "house-keeping".

I am the type of person who likes to go forward and do new things. But every now and then it is very important to look back at what we have currently. If you keep on going forward without taking care of your business support in terms of your website, product, customers and so on, it is just a matter of time before you "crash".

There is always free and targeted traffic right under my nose that I don't realize until I do my own "house-keeping".

For example, I can easily update a few of my eBooks and free reports with a new link to my other new products like The Freedom Formula Coaching Program. When I do this, I am able to generate more traffic effortlessly by simply putting an additional link in my old or existing eBooks.

Other than that, I can just add a "Recommendation" link to the new site that I need traffic for on my current website that is getting decent traffic.

One of the most effective ways I use to "recycle" my traffic is by using pop ups. There are special pop up software programs specifically designed to help you get better results.

So you see, when you do "house-keeping", you will realize you are really wasting a lot of traffic if you do not know how to "recycle" it. Instead of visiting one website or online business of yours, the same visitor can visit 5 of your other websites if you know how to direct them properly. You will never know which website will hit the visitor's hot button to buy from you.

16. THE INTERNET HAS STOP WORKING?

If you're making a lot of money on the internet right now, then this article is not for you to read. But otherwise, read this entirely so that you get the bigger picture of what's wrong and start making money online, very quickly.

You see, there's an endless loop thing going on in the internet marketing niche. The endless loop is this - an 'internet marketer' teaches how to make money online by selling how to make money online stuff and that is how he makes money online. I know it becomes a cliché, but try to analyze what I mean by that.

There's nothing wrong with that because it's not cheating but it's a vicious cycle that is actually, totally hollow.

THE BIGGEST PROBLEM IS, they make outrageous promises which in reality, won't happen to a Newbie because a Newbie wouldn't be able to market in the internet marketing niche right away. I'll tell you why - to be in the internet marketing niche, **you must understand internet marketing.**

Secondly, you've got to have your own success to convince people to buy and lastly, you need Joint Venture partners. A Newbie probably doesn't has any of these (that's why we use the word, Newbie.)

Yeah, you can get a sale or two by doing Adwords selling your own internet marketing course but if you really want to do a reality check, you probably sell nothing because you'll be competing with other best-sellers when you bid for the keyword, 'internet marketing course'.

Of course, you can bypass this process by writing a super sales letter to SELL and don't really bother about people's success and sell junk. That's why you see there is plenty of garbage out there and yet they sell very well because it's a good sales letter and they're good at marketing to do a product launch.

So the Newbie wonders why the Internet doesn't work, or has stopped working.

That's not true because the Internet is actually doing well, very well indeed, even in economy downturn.

The missing puzzle is getting into the 'right' market when a Newbie is first starting.

I encourage anyone to go into the 'internet marketing' niche because it's such a lucrative market for you to make a lot of money, but don't do that until you really understand how internet marketing works and have success to display.

The advice here is dead simple - if you're a Newbie, get into an easy niche market and start make your first $1,000. Forget everything else, for now. Whether it's selling a course teaching frogs to jump higher or how to fix a smiling face, doesn't matter - what matters is getting it RIGHT first and get it moving. Then it's so much easier to roll out more things **once you know what you need to know.**

The other concern is info-overload.

You can get 'overload' or sick if you eat too much. That's call overeating. Or over-exhausted if you exercise too much.

There's no such thing as info-overload. I mean, your stomach has only a limited space and you can just fit that much food in it or you only have limited calories to burn when exercising. Your brain doesn't have a limit, it's not like it's a computer with a preset memory capacity.

I know, I know... I know what you mean by info-overload. I'm just trying to make a point that scientifically, you cannot get info-overload because there's no real limit and you can decide how to 'control' your brain.

In my opinion, **you will experience info-overload if you have lack of focus.**

Like, why are you reading a course about making money with Google Adsense right now if you're trying to make money online by selling an info-product?

Perhaps you don't, but MOST NEWBIES DO. *They want to learn everything.*

I acknowledge the attitude of having great learning desire but if you can't handle too many things, then eliminate the rest and just do one.

That ONE will give you a result, which in this, will turn into money for you.

Don't worry about losing out on the latest 'trend' or hot stuff - they're temporary and something else will pop up again next month, okay?

Get into the right niche market today.

Note: Depending on when you're reading this book, I've made a 4-week affiliate marketing home course available for newbies to start – it's at:

www.patricchan.net/affiliatemarketing

17. THE TECHNIQUE TO PRICE YOUR EBOOK

So, let's say you have your own eBook. Now you have to decide how much to charge for it. Finding the right price is essential to the success of your product in terms of how profitable it can be.

If you charge too little, people will think it is of little value, and they won't purchase it. Or even if they did, you will have to sell thousands of copies to get to the point where you can begin to see a huge profit. But that does not really matter because with the correct marketing strategies, you can definitely sell a lot of copies.

If you price your eBook too high when compared to your competitors, you will find yourself in a nasty competition. Of course if you lose, you end up with nothing in your pocket.

Another problem with selling your eBook at a high price is you will have a tough time reducing it in the near future. For example, if you were to sell your eBook at first for $47.00 and later reduce it to $27.00, don't you think the people who bought it for $47.00 are going to be unhappy and disappointed, or maybe even angry with you?

So the "first rule" of pricing eBooks is to *never underprice.*

The price should be aimed at bringing in profits, but you should never forget that price is one of the factors that people use in judging the value of your eBook before they buy it. So always start with the lowest price that you can still make a healthy profit and then increase it gradually if there is a good demand for it.

Pricing an eBook is particularly difficult because they are intangible products. Since they are in digital form, the value of an eBook is as confusing as the understanding of what digital actually is to the average layperson. That is why you are selling its *PERCEIVED VALUE.*

Your eBook is actually information. It is the information in these books that has the ability to change, or possibly transform, people's lives. People are looking for solutions. It is the information that is valuable! That is how you determine the price of your eBook.

If your eBook contains valuable, and more importantly, new information, references or techniques, then you should aim to price it on the high end. For example, does your book solve a particular problem? If it does, and solves it in a way that hasn't been written about in one hundred other eBooks, you will be able to achieve high sales at a high price.

Just make sure the question or problem that your eBook solves is important and relevant to the majority of your targeted audience. If your ideas are not common knowledge, or you are presenting a brand-new technique, you will be able to sell your eBook at a high price. Just be prepared for your competition to undercut you on price as soon as they hear about your product.

If your eBook is aimed at solving one particular problem rather than general advice, then you can charge more. An effective technique for figuring out a price is to send out a survey to your current customers or subscribers. If these customers have already bought an eBook from you, ask for their opinion in terms of price. Of course, the results can be biased.

Lastly, the price for your eBook also depends on the online niche business.

For example, you can sell for a higher price in the "how to make money" niche market. I have seen eBooks that sold for $97 teaching the reader how to make money from the internet, etc., but I have never seen an eBook teaching dog owners to be better dog trainers for that same price. The general rule here is, you can make more money if you have a product, in this case an eBook, that helps others make more money.

18. THE SECRET TO SELLING AN "IDEA" ONLINE

What is an "offer"? It is simply your value proposition. In other words, what you are prepared to give your customers in exchange for their money.

Each time you send a product promotion to your mailing list or post a product to sell on your websites, those are all offers. You see, if you ask people for money, you actually have to give them something in return. Logically, no one is going to give you money for free.

So the key to making this work is by delivering something that has a *high perceived* value which actually costs you less than the product's selling price. That is how you make a profit; that is how all businesses make profits, just in case you didn't know!

Generally, making money means selling a product. Take the sales amount minus your product cost and the remainder is your profit. This is simple to understand, isn't it? Yet, some people can't get the equation right!

The difference between your cost and the *selling price* which someone is willing to pay for your product is *profit*. When I say "profit" I usually mean gross *profit*. You still have to deduct your fixed and variable expenses as well as taxes before arriving at your *net profit*.

From this point onwards, unless I state otherwise, I am only talking about gross profit.

The Most Profitable Product Is...

There is no other product on the face of this earth with higher profitability than *information*. In many cases, especially online, your gross profit on an information product is 100 per cent--you can't get much higher than that!

However, there are some unique problems with selling information products that do not occur when selling other types of products.

The first problem is that you cannot take a picture of them. The only way to describe them is through your words -- your sales copy, the text or video describing your product. And unlike their physical counterparts, eBooks and digital products do not even exist in the "real world" because they are electrons.

But truthfully, what you are selling is what those electrons represent, which are "ideas", correct?

So those electrons are no longer just that but they are "ideas" now. Therefore when you sell an information product of any kind, digital or paper based, you are actually selling "ideas".

Those "ideas" are just the beginning, though. You cannot sell "ideas" just like that, can you?

Let's say you tell the world that you have this great idea, but you don't tell them what it was, and you are willing to sell this "idea" to the first buyer for $49. Do you think it would sell? Probably not. (But you can never know. Strangely, some people will buy!)

Now, if you said, I have an idea on "how to make $1 million dollars" and you tried selling it for $49, you would probably get many more buyers now, wouldn't you?

Nonetheless again, if you had sold your idea *without* a detailed explanation, you are going to get refund requests for those sales. This is because not every customer will find your great idea suitable for them.

Generic ideas or answers will not make you rich. Like I said, even if you sell a lot of those, you will get refund requests.

And Now, For The Rest Of The Story...

What you need are *detailed ideas or new ideas* to convince your prospects to pay you money for them without asking for refunds. Wow, how novel, eh?

Let me elaborate on what detailed ideas and new ideas are.

A *generic* idea of making money from the stock market is to buy the stock when the price is low and selling it when it is high.

Detailed ideas are those that tell the speculators *exactly how* they can buy low and sell high. Also, you might want to include the procedures to do this.

New ideas are those that tell them how they can make money from the stock market without buying low and selling high. For instance, how to get the stocks for free and selling them when they are listed. Now, I don't think it is possible to get stocks for free... but if it were possible, isn't that a new idea? If you have these new ideas and they do actually work, you can expect to sell a lot of them on the internet.

Customers are looking for details and new ideas — *not* just ideas, even though that is what you told them they would get.

How To Do This Profitably

If you want to hit home-runs when selling your ideas, *include* the details in your product that they never expected to find.

Give your customers *more* than just an "idea"; give them more details, *more* information and *more* advice than they thought they were going to get! And most of all, give them *new ideas*!

Think creatively how to sell your idea when you have one in mind. Remember, detailed and new ideas.

19. HOW ARE YOU GOING TO MAKE MONEY ONLINE?

By selling products online, of course! Actually, that is just a surface answer.

You will need to sell a product to make money. But there are many types of products you can sell. Not only that, there are many ways, too. What do I mean?

Good question! I was just getting into that. Now, "selling a product" online could mean the following:

1.   Be an affiliate marketer to sell someone's product;
2.   Selling your own tangible products;
3.   Selling your own info-products;
4.   "Selling" Google Adsense;
5.   "Selling" website traffic;
6.   Selling dropship products;
7.   Selling public domain products;
8.   ... and many more!

There are also many ways to achieve your desired results. You could:

1.   Try to get ranked high in a search engine like Google.com and leverage on its traffic;
2.   Advertise using Google Adwords;
3.   Post on auction sites like eBay.com;
4.   Contact JV partners;
5.   Buy solo ads to advertise in ezines;
6.   Create a "Fire Sale";
7.   Social media promotion;
8.   ... and many more!

Are you starting to get my point?

There are lots of ways to make money on the internet. And yet, sometimes it is hard to achieve that. Do you want to know why?

You need to focus on one way to make money first! Yes, focus! On one! Once you have done that successfully, then you can consider other alternatives.

For instance, let's say you had received some emails on how to make money from eBay. Because the product is supposed to be that good, you bought it. And guess what? It is that good! But, it still takes some time to make your first dollar from it.

Then suddenly, you receive another email next week on how to make money from affiliate programs by getting your site ranked on page one of Google.com. So you bought it as well. And this goes on and on... with you "investing" your money like the proverbial headless chicken, running everywhere without aim --and still not making money.

My advice in this situation is, don't try something new unless the other products recommended are related to eBay.com (which was your original foray).

FOCUS

Let's say you buy 10 eBooks on how to make money from eBay. That is fine because you are focusing on one way. But if you were to buy and read 3 eBooks on search engines, one eBook on joint venture marketing, three on eBay and three more on creating your own membership sites, it is going to take a longer time for you to make money, this I can guarantee you.

All you need is to *focus on* one. In fact, I don't make money from eBay or search engines. Here is my strategy:

1. Create a profitable webpage;
2. Then attract traffic;
3. Convert the traffic to sales;
4. Apply back-end sales; and
5. Automate the business.

If you just focus on one, it should not take you too much time to earn money online. Then afterwards you can use other strategies to complement it. For instance, if you plan to sell affiliate products by getting listed in search engines, then you can consider learning about RSS and blogs because those will help you get a ranking in the search engines. But don't go and buy any software on how to create an eBook cover!

Got my point?

20. THE 4-STEP WRITING FORMULA

Whether you're writing an article or a fully fledged book, I got the formula for you...

Step One: Write Out A List of Everything You Want To Share. That's right, just write down everything you want to share in your writing. I'm talking just start rambling on paper (or your computer screen). Everything you can think of that relates to the subject of your eBook. Just a list of "ideas" you want to share.

Step Two: Write Everything You Can Think Of For Each Entry. For each entry on your list (I.E. Each "idea") write down everything you can think of. Explain each idea as thoroughly as you can. Share research, examples, case studies, quotes, tips, resources -- everything you can find for each section.

Step Three: Organize Your Thoughts. Take everything and put it into a logical order. If it's a tutorial, organize it chronologically in order of which steps come first. If it's a "tips" eBook, categorize the tips. Put things in a logical order for your readers to be able to understand as they begin reading.

Step Four: Edit And Pad The Sections. Go back to each section and edit. Take out what doesn't need to be in there. Add more content to the sections that need further explanation.

Congratulations. You have just learned the 4-step writing formula.

21. WHAT I LEARNED FROM BUYING A PAIR OF GLASSES

I lost my new glasses. Without them, I found it rather difficult to work, so I got another pair.

Before I bought my new glasses, I had two choices:

An unbranded pair costing US $20.

A pair of Oakley glasses costing US $159. (Just in case you do not know about Oakley, here is their official site: www.oakley.com. They are one of the best when it comes to sunglasses.)

By the way, the design of the "unbranded" first option looked exactly like the Oakley's which I wanted. Guess what? I ended up buying the Oakley, even though it was 8 times more expensive! ... *And I am a happy customer.*

Do you want to know why I bought the Oakley?

All Oakley glasses come with warranty. If somehow my glasses got broken, they won't charge me to replace them with a new pair.

There are many celebrities wearing and endorsing them. They receive tons of honors and positive feedback from reliable third party sources like *Men's Health, Times Online Edition, Fortune, Business Week Online* and *USA Today's Sports. You* will also see Oakleys in many movies like in *Mission Impossible* (worn by Tom Cruise) and *Transformers.*

Oakley is "branded". A well-known brand makes you feel "cool" wearing it. The branding is so powerful that you feel a sense of belonging, that you are an owner of Oakley eyewear.

Oakley has superior quality. If I am not mistaken, they claim to have the best sunglass lenses on Earth. That is a huge claim, but wouldn't you feel 10 times safer when wearing them with this kind of claim?

From the way how I was convinced to buy them, I realized that the same marketing strategies can be applied on the internet. In fact, most internet marketing experts are already using them!

For instance:

Warranty. Can you offer a guarantee on the products that you are currently selling? If you can, offer a longer period of guarantee. Don't just do 30 days. Offer one year or something like that. That is how you show customers how confident you are of your products and that you are not in business just because you are desperate for their money. Testimonials and endorsements. Do your products or websites have these? It is important to get familiar names giving a green light that your products are good. If your products are mentioned in articles and so on, those are credibility boosts.

Even internet marketers can be "branded". Consumers prefer to buy from well-known internet marketers with proven results. For example, if Donald Trump wanted to do internet marketing, I think people will attend his internet marketing seminar because he is "branded". John Smith may have the same talent, knowledge, ideas and presentation skills like Donald, but John might not be able to sell as many seats as Donald because he has not yet built up his "brand-name" yet. The good news is, if John *perseveres*, his credibility will grow. One day he too will be able to sell easily.

Does your product offer valuable content? Can you offer any claims with proof to back it up? For instance, your eBook doesn't have to be the most comprehensive search engine guide, but if you were to work and think hard, I guess you could come up with a reasonably good and helpful "How To Find Linking Partners for Newbies" guide!

So the next time you buy something at the shopping mall, think carefully whether you are under the influence of powerful marketing strategies. We all are most times -- it is just that we were not aware of it!

22. I USE THIS MARKETING STRATEGY

I want to share with you a very valuable marketing lesson today -- the "Reason Why" strategy.

Let me share with you a quick story – years ago, I released a product called, The *Publishing Business Secrets DVD* course. I sold 73 copies in less than 18 hours from 722 visitors visiting the webpage.

The product was sold at US$397 per package at the pre-launch price. So, that is an average of US$40.14 per website visitor.

Do you want to know why it converted so well?

The "Reason Why" strategy was one of the main reasons -- no pun intended. This strategy basically communicates with your prospects the "reason" why they need to order it today without any delay. In a nutshell, you need to give a compelling reason why your prospects should buy from you today.

It sounds very simple but the strategy is way more powerful than it sounds.

Why?

Because the strategy taps into one of a human being's most powerful decision-makers, that is, a feeling of urgency to take immediate action.

So you must create urgency in your offer.

The best "reason" to use in this strategy is to create a limited offer. Limited offers can be any or a combination of these:

The price will increase later;

Get extra bonus products if they buy now;

Limited stocks available;

A special payment plan if they take up the offer now; etc.

Whatever you do, please do not use poor "reasons" for this strategy. I have seen some marketers using the reason of "running out of seats" when they are selling webinars! How is that even logical? This strategy is fine if you sincerely want, for instance, only 50 people to attend your call. But if you are trying to pack it with as many participants as possible, don't use this "reason".

In my personal opinion, nevertheless, this is not a good "reason why" strategy. Would you believe it if someone were to tell you that it is not possible to increase the lines for more participants to a call? Maybe that is true, who knows, maybe they really cannot extend more lines due to cost considerations or technological limitations.

However, if you are selling a real live seminar, it is okay to use the "reason" of limited seats because your venue might only be able to seat a certain number of people. Or sometimes you do want to make sure the crowd is not too big so that you have better control or have a more productive Q&A session.

Another "reason" that makes no sense is that the product will be sold out when you are selling an eBook! An eBook is just a digital document. It is not logical to tell people that it can be "sold out"! That is, unless you have said that the information is so special that you only want to sell 100 copies of it because you do not want to share the content with the world. Then that "reason" is fine. But do make absolute sure you keep your words or it will backfire, and you will lose all your credibility, reputation and goodwill.

I have seen marketers who sold limited copies of their eBooks with great success. And the reason why? "Never to sell it to the public again."

When you use the "reason why" strategy, it has to be valid and logical. Your explanation and plan has to make sense.

In a recent promotion, by using the "reason why" strategy, I stressed that we had limited quantities of a certain new eBook. The "reason" was valid because we had only produced 100 copies to "test" the market and to get feedback. And it was the truth because after the 100 copies were sold, I stopped selling it. Skeptical customers who did not believe me placed orders but we said we had no more... until we do a new version.

Remember, a customer's decision to buy is influenced by the emotion and justified by the logical mind. So always have a good "reason" why your prospects should buy from you --and buy from you *today*!

23. IT'S SUNDAY

Read this chapter and stop working. Yes, you read that right. After reading this chapter, go out and smell the roses. If you have kids, play with them. If your Dad or Mum is around, go talk with them. If you have a wife or husband, go kiss and hug her or him because you want to do that.

Or just pamper yourself and watch TV. Like playing some sports? Go play.

Do whatever you want right now that you like. Be present and enjoy your life right now.

I am writing this because I was working a few minutes ago. I saw my parents sitting there watching TV. The sky was so beautiful and I could just imagine dipping myself in my swimming pool on this sunny day. My friends are probably out playing sports.

But I am working today -- Sunday.

For what?

For my future. I know I am not working for my past or present moment. I am working for my future by exchanging my present pleasure time. But even if I don't work anymore, honestly, I will have enough money to spend for years because I am financially free today.

So, I am going to stop working just for today and enjoy myself.

And so must you. That is why I am writing this.

Be present today. Relax. Chill out.

I am not asking you to be lazy. Be consistently hard-working but spare some time to have fun and enjoy your life. Just for today. Go back to work tomorrow.

But for today, be with the people you love. Do the things you like to do. If you are on a diet, scrap that. Go and taste the ice-cream you want. Hmm...

How does that feel?

I just wrote this chapter because I felt like telling you something important. It was not about trying to impress anyone with words like "chill out" or "go out and smell the roses" or to not-so-subtly remind you how rich and successful I am -- really, but to encourage you to have a wonderful and wholesome life.

And ... if you are reading this chapter on Monday, Tuesday, Wednesday, etc. you still have the time to have fun when you finish your work today. Don't miss that. Your loved ones are waiting for you...

Okay. I am done.

24. THE BEST WAY TO SELL YOUR PRODUCT

Do you want to know the best way to sell your product that will almost guarantee you to make money online?

Get a joint venture partner in your same niche market to promote your product to his mailing list. I can bet you will see sales in less than 24 hours if it is a quality JV partner. My previous JV partner generated US$21,492 in sales in just a couple of days, by just mailing to his list!

Anyway, I said it is the best way, but I didn't say it is the easiest way. In fact, it is one of the toughest ways to achieve this kind of success. But it is very rewarding.

Getting someone to consider promoting your product is a lot of work. Please do read and reread the other chapters where I share on joint venture partnerships. In this chapter I want to tell you how to avoid the big mistakes to maximize your results.

Most people send out joint venture proposals to the wrong JV partners and end up being disappointed. I know this because I receive a lot of JV proposals.

If you are a long-time subscriber of mine, you will notice that I hardly promote or endorse any third party products. The reason is most times the proposals do not meet my criteria. I simply will not endorse non-useful products to my subscribers--not even if I am paid 100 per cent commission. This is because it is crucial that the products recommended at this particular site of mine are those that will help my subscribers make money online.

Competing Vs Complementing Products

The other major mistake I have seen is people trying to have joint ventures with partners who have a directly competing product--rather than one complementing theirs! For example, I have a course about Facebook marketing. So, what is the possibility of me promoting someone else's Facebook marketing course?

Rarely, unless there are other perks involved. But let's say the major influence of considering the offer is to make affiliate commissions. It would be my last priority to promote a product that belongs to my direct competitor and whose ideas are in conflict with what I am teaching!

Yet most people approach JV partners to promote a product that is competing with that prospective partner's existing product. That is incredibly unwise to say the least.

So what kind of products might I want to promote that complement those that I have?

In this case, I might consider promoting Twitter training to my subscribers since I am teaching social media marketing. Or maybe, software to create video for Facebook and Youtube marketing. Basically, I will consider promoting products that are complementary, not competing.

So seek JV partners who have complementary products to yours. Like, if you are selling a blogging software, your ideal JV partners would be people who sell courses on how to make money online from blogging. Makes sense?

In this case, I would be able to sell some blogging software as a JV partner of yours. Nevertheless, you will definitely get better results by contacting a more targeted partner. You see, the efforts you have to put in are the same. So why not approach a more qualified partner like someone who is in the "How to Blog" niche?

You still want to approach as many JV partners as possible, but start with the more targeted potential partners first because those will be more effective.

Let me give you another example so that you can relate -- if your eBook's title is *77 Ways To Potty Train Your Dog*, your most suitable and quality JV partner would be the author of *How To Train Your Dog To Sit And Fetch*. Why? Because his customers would most likely be interested in your eBook!

Of course, this concept may not be applicable if there are other influences or factors involved. These could be long-standing relationships, high affiliate commissions, 2-way JV swaps, unique products, additional benefits, free product access, etc.

You see, finding a complementing product is just one of the important keys of selecting a JV partner successfully. When other influences are in the picture, a product or website owner might even consider promoting a competing product. This is normal, whether with online or regular brick-and-mortar business.

Think Big But...

Another tip about seeking joint ventures is, start small if you are just starting out. Do not approach the "Big Boys" of your niche market yet when you are new, no matter how tempting it is.

Get the ball rolling first, because if you spoil your first impression when you approach them, you will risk losing the opportunity to do business with them forever. Get a few small deals done first and you will be more motivated and inspired to keep it growing.

Then, and only then, go to "Big Boys" and offer them a win-win deal.

25. ONLINE INTEGRITY: DOES IT EXIST?

Integrity is what sets you apart from your competitors and makes your customers want to order your great products again.

I want to take this opportunity to talk a little bit about online integrity. Does it exist anymore?

It is sad to say, you have to be extra careful nowadays because there are marketers who do not have integrity and they can hide behind the computer. For instance, I have promoted products and never received affiliate commissions. I have purchased products and never received emails from the merchant again when I was not satisfied with the products. I have done article swaps, eBook swaps, endorsement swaps, but never got the reciprocal swap from my JV partners.

Do I complain?

Nope. I just kept quiet and learned from my mistakes. Of course, I will email to those dubious people first to solve the problems. But after two or three times and still not getting any response from them, I will no longer put in any effort to resolve those problems. ... It is just a matter of time before their whole business collapses.

So, how are you going to avoid these people?

You can't. My simple guideline is this: if you are buying a "how to make money" or an internet marketing course, stay with real-name marketers so that you know they will want to deliver quality information.

But what if you got burned while trying something new? Well, then you get to learn valuable lessons in return! And I am not trying be mean when I say this. For instance, here are some which I have learnt:

1. Don't ever do this to anyone else on the internet. You know how it feels. If you cannot offer a JV swap, just say you can't. People will respect you more that way. Do not promise someone else and become a big, fat, greedy leech using other people.

2. You will improve yourself from the mistakes you have made.

3. You will not be cheated by these same people again, and this might save you a lot of time and money in the future.

I once promoted an online MLM program* and never received any affiliate commission. And they also never replied my emails about my problem. But I am "happy" that I was cheated because these people created more programs subsequently, and since now I know, I don't associate with these people again. Lucky for me that I discovered their lack of integrity early before helping them to build a larger organization!

Secondly, I am now smarter when it comes to picking other MLM programs to promote in the future -- those that are truly worthwhile, genuine, profitable and trustworthy.

Never whine. Just learn, be thankful and go on building your business.

* If you're interested to know what MLM business I'm currently involved with, go to **www.patricchan.net/networkmarketing**

26. STRAIGHTFORWARD ADVICE -- NO BS

If you are not succeeding in what you want to achieve, it is because you are thinking or *analyzing* too much about what you should do instead of just doing it! Frankly, you have no one else to blame except yourself. It is your fault. Just like it was my fault for being poor and working a job I hated. I chose it -- nobody pointed a gun at my head!

That was last time. Now, I choose my life to be the way I want.

Every day you choose what you do with your time, your day. No one forces you to work a job you hate or be poor. I know, this is hard to take, but it is the truth.

I am not saying you should not take your time and *plan* what you are going to do. But once you have decided what you really, really want, to make more money, and you are really, really tired of being poor... then make that plan and take action! Then do not stop but follow through with your plan until you succeed.

Basically the world is divided between 2 kinds of people -- the *doers* and the *talkers*. Which are you -- a doer or a talker?

A talker usually complains, blames others and justifies his or her situation.

Be a doer. Success comes to those who take what they want by doing something right that gets them closer to their goals each day. Even if you made a wrong decision, doing something is still better than doing nothing--because this is how we learn to be better! Falling down is not the problem; not walking at all or not getting up when you fall is!

You will never hear anyone else say this in the same way that I do, but it is

100 per cent true: Nothing, and I mean nothing, beats persistence!

You can be stupid, poor and ugly, but if you are persistent enough about working towards what you want, meaning you are *focused*, you will *succeed* -- period! You will succeed online.

If you do *nothing else* the rest of this year, just implement this one simple piece of personal advice I am giving you right now. You will gain more working knowledge, more confidence, more experience, more credibility, more good reputation... and yes, more success.

27. QUICK MONEY VS SLOW MONEY

A lot of people jump on the internet bandwagon hoping to make money online. This is a good choice because I strongly believe it is easier to start a business online than offline. And the opportunity online is just so huge!

The first thing you need to do is make up your mind on whether you are looking for "quick money" or "slow money".

Get this: *neither* is bad or good. Both options are good. Both will put money into your pocket. They are just how they are and each option has a different method to achieve success. Understanding what you are going after is more important to get the results you want.

So, are you looking for quick money or slow money online?

I can understand that most people would want to gain quick money. I mean, who wants to wait to see an income from the internet -- duh! The faster it is, the better, isn't it? Well, the thing is, generally, slow money will provide a more consistent and stable income for you. If you are planning to retire or quit your job with your internet income, then go for the slow money option.

Honestly, you can earn quick money online as fast as within 24 hours. Here is how to do it...

The Speedy Gonzales Style

Pick a product that you want to promote as an affiliate. If you don't know where to find products to promote as an affiliate, the easiest place to find them is at Clickbank.com. Once you have it, go and buy some pay-per-click advertising at Google Adwords or Facebook Advertising. You are in business in less than 24 hours. Will you make money or not? It really depends on your marketing skill by then.

That is *quick money*! The problem with quick money is, you are not really building a business for yourself. You are making money, but not building a business. However, unfortunately, building a business does not necessarily mean that you are making money.

Another way of making quick money is by buying solo ads in a newsletter to promote an affiliate product that you know is converting very well.

All very straightforward, right? Now, let's go "slow-mo" and...

Move As Fast As A Glacier

A slow money strategy is focused on building an asset for your business.

Some of the strategies include spending months to get high rankings in search engines, creating your own brand, building relationships with JV partners, etc.

If you cannot decide whether you want quick or slow money from the internet, just ask yourself this: "Do I want to build a business or just want to make money?"

I will say do *both*, but focus more on "slow money" because it will pay off many times better. The "quick money" will help you to pay off your current bills while your "slow money" will give you peace of mind each night when you sleep. Small sacrifices but huge rewards.

The best way to explain this concept is by using the "Hunter or Farmer" analogy.

A *hunter* wakes up to hunt for food to eat every day. If he does not get any animals that day, he will have nothing to eat.

A *farmer* plants vegetables and fruits for food. But during the period between planting and harvesting, he will have nothing to eat.

So, be *both--a* hunter and a farmer.

28. QUIT BEFORE YOU HAVE A CHANCE TO SUCCEED?

It is sometimes funny when you look back at your own accomplishments and the whole journey you took towards your current success. But "funnier" still is, many people do not complete what they start because they mentally and emotionally conclude early in their journey that "this can't work".

In the past, I was totally not focused and easily distracted. After achieving some success on the internet, I took it for granted and went on to do something else before I fully realized the potential of the business I had started.

In my early days, I sold Anthony Robbins Seminar tickets. At the same time, I tried to make money by joining and promoting multilevel marketing products. Then, I also got involved in selling some e-learning stuff to college students and company employees. Finally, while still doing all those, I started my own seminar-organizing business and partnered with speakers.

An uninformed person reading this might say that I was very enterprising and being a real go-getter. But the truth is, I was totally unfocused... and it cost me a lot! Both time and money.

For 2 years after starting my business I struggled... almost to the point of being in debt. Actually, I was in debt.

Good thing I did not give up -- or else the whole thing would have just collapsed on me!

Now, this chapter is not about me. There is a very pertinent message I am trying to convey to you.

Have you given yourself the chance to be successful?

You might be struggling right now, who knows. If that is the case, do not quit before you have the chance to succeed... if you truly believe in what you are doing.

You see, there is a difference between being persistent and being stupid.

Let's put it this way: you have to quit if you have to quit. But do not ever think of quitting if you know that you can be successful.

So the million-dollar question is: How do you know whether the goal you are pursuing can be successful or not?

Well, *success leaves clues.*

A simple way to know is by judging from the results which other people are getting by doing the same things that you are doing! Plain and simple. If your business model has almost the same characteristics as those of the successful people, that is a good "clue" that you are on the right track, and that you should be persistent.

Remember, success leaves clues.

29. SOME TIPS ABOUT CREATING AN INFO-PRODUCT

We all have problems, don't we? Products and services are there to help us solve those problems.

Your products created are the solutions to problems. So when there is a problem, there is an opportunity for you to make money -- whether online or offline.

Nevertheless, sometimes, when you have discovered a problem, there is already a product created to solve it. So what? Does that mean that you no longer have the opportunity to tap into this problem? Says who? Just make your product better, faster, cleaner, more reliable, more cost effective, better presented... well, you get the idea.

If you look at the bright side, it means there are a lot of people who are willing to pay to get their problems solved.

Don't get me wrong -- I am not telling you to go out, buy other people's stuff, clone it, give it a fancy new name and change the layout a bit and then sell it! Aside from probably getting yourself into trouble with copyright laws and such, it is just not practical or ethical.

What I am showing you, though, is that you can take basic ideas, and you can make them a better solution to a specific problem from the ground up. Be innovative.

You will find all kinds of products at Clickbank.com's Marketplace. There are plenty of info-products for you to look through there.

No matter how weird or crazy your product idea seems, no matter why you think it won't work, don't give it up. Never call it quits before you give deep consideration on how it can be *successful*. You will never know whether that idea could be your big money-maker one day.

Open your mind a little, and don't start dismissing things on a whim because they seem impractical or even impossible at first glance. Sometimes it has a lot to do with your lack of self-confidence. Sometimes it could be your own limited perception of things.

Some of your ideas may look impractical when you list them down. It may seem like there is no market for them or you can't afford to create them. But, always keep an open mind and don't start placing these limits on yourself before you even start!

Once we remove those limits, the ideas will begin flowing. Start recording them. One of them may well be the next big thing in your field of expertise. You can sort out the good from the not-so-good ideas later.

Then, after listing your ideas, evaluate them.

I will admit, as a newbie, it could be hard to start creating info-products, but once you settle into this idea of bringing new concepts to the front of your mind and exploring them, you will see that things will become possible -- and you will never run out of ideas for new products!

There are 4 types of formats you can use to create an info-product: eBooks, software, audios and videos. The easiest and fastest way is to record an audio product. Then, transcribe it and you will have the eBook version immediately.

If you can't create an audio product by yourself, interview an expert, or two, in your niche market. I am sure many people would want to learn from them.

How can you convince them to be interviewed?

Do a teleconference call to promote their product as an affiliate to your mailing list and record it. They won't be able to resist that.

Software and video info-products are slightly more complex to create. The reason why both these info-products are being created by marketers very often lately is because of the high perceived value they can sell it for.

"Is there a market for my product?"

And can you reach your targeted prospective customers?

Two very important questions indeed, because incidentally, if there is no market for your product or you have no way to reach your customers, you simply won't sell any.

It is easy enough to head over to Google.com and do a search for your product or a different version of it. In your search, if you do find that there are other products out there that are similar to yours, you can bet your life that there is a market out there!

Specifics and how-tos aren't really important right now. Just understand enough not to go launching a product that has no demand or which is going to be impossible for you to reach the prospective buyers.

30. THE ADVANTAGE OF NICHE MARKETING

Do you know what the most common question is that I get about internet marketing? The one, by far, which most newbies and interested individuals ask me? It is this:

"How do I make money on the internet?"

Now, I want to be honest with you. It is a logical and valid question... but it is one that is literally impossible to answer because there are just too many things to talk about on that topic!

I mean, other analogies to that question would be: "How can you make a girl/guy like you?" or "How can I be a good parent?"

There are so many different ways to achieve them!

But, if I could sum it all up to give you the secret of making money online fast *without* competing with experienced internet marketing gurus, the answer is:

"Build an online niche business."

What, an online niche business? What is that, you ask.

It is niche marketing, friends. For the record, I will define an online niche business as a business that is not about "How To" make money online or offline and internet marketing-related topics.

Let me clarify by mentioning a different few niche marketing examples:

o A website about dog training;
o A website about digital cameras;
o A website about wedding planning;
o A website about babysitting;
o A website about fresh water fishing;

o A website about Thai kickboxing; etc.

Do you get the idea now?

However, I have to agree with you that the "How To" make money niche market is a profitable market indeed -- no doubt about that. People who are serious about making more money are always more willing to invest to learn more so they can earn more. They don't play "hokey-pokey", i.e. do things with double mindedness.

So, why am I still insisting that everyone who has asked me how to make money online should explore the income potential of niche marketing? Am I afraid of competitors? That is silly. Does Anthony Robbins worry about the other thousands of motivational speakers in the United States?

I don't think so.

The reason I highly recommend someone to build a niche business is because he or she will not be competing head-on with experienced internet marketing gurus. It would be like racing in the Formula One circuit driving your family car.

For example, if you are planning to build a niche market for martial arts, you could focus on "ninjitsu for women" or something like that. Just don't try and build a so-called niche market on "martial arts". That is too huge of a market.

Now, how many experienced internet marketing gurus are you going to be competing with at "ninjitsu for women"? Hardly any, probably. But hey, please don't go and do this yet! That is just an example that I plucked from the sky. Do plenty of research first.

But here is the most important advice: It is not about making $100,000 from a niche market, or whatever amount of money you set yourself to earn. It is how you are going to make the first $1 from that niche. Once you have done that successfully, there is nothing stopping you from improving that online niche business' income.

Let's talk about "ninjitsu for women" again.

The first product that you sell might be an eBook titled, 10 Easy Ways To *Master Ninjitsu Martial Arts* For Women. Once you sell that, you could expand your niche business and start selling:

1.   More ebooks;
2.   Ninjitsu tools and gear (Sell as an affiliate to reduce the handling inventory and order fulfilment costs);

3.   Ninjitsu classes; etc.

The sky is the limit for what else you can sell in the same niche market, as long as you know how to make your first dollar online.

Are you excited about the huge possibility?

31. THE INTERNET MARKETING EPIPHANY

It was an epiphany when I realized the 3 basic rules to make a lot of money on the internet as below. And weirdly enough, I wasn't seeking them, they just "popped up" from my recent experiences...

1. Recently, I wrote a new eBook called WakeUp Millionaire and it was selling well. So I was about to move to the next project, but then it "caught" me - why am I moving to the next project when this is proven to make money!!??

If it's making money, all I need to do is to focus on promoting it even more. So here's the first epiphany for making lots of money on the internet: all you need to do is send more traffic to *something* that is already converting traffic to cash. And seriously, you cannot be giving the excuse of not knowing HOW to get traffic because traffic is always readily available to be purchased.

2. I was brainstorming with my partner the other day on the many ways of generating profits from sales funnel. We thought of a great product to offer to our customers. Needless to say, I was excited with the whole strategy. But then, it hit me - why am I thinking of new sales funnel when we don't even have many customers yet!!??

Epiphany #2 - don't be bothered about increasing revenue if you haven't generated sufficient revenue yet. To me, it's a complete waste of time because the same amount of time can be focused on marketing instead.

3. The last epiphany is this -- it's almost a science when it comes to making money on the internet. Here's the "science":

i. Find a market.
ii. Put up a webpage to get them to subscribe to a mailing list
iii. Drive traffic to this webpage
iv. Send out emails with offers related to what the market wants. You can never run out of offers because there are so many affiliate networks

around. For instance, go to *www.clickbank.com* for pay-per-sale or *www.peerflynet.com* for pay-per-lead offers.

Where people go wrong with making lots of money on the internet are…

1. At first, they make a sale or some small amount of money online. And because it wasn't a big pay check, they simply give up. What they didn't understand is, the "first year" was supposedly spent to build a strong foundation so that they can leap later on. You crawl before you walk, and you walk before you run.

2. They do so much freaking research! And sometimes, the funniest part is, they're researching for evidence why the methods won't work and intended instead they intend to find a "better" way. Gosh.

3. The formula is already right in front of their face. Dude, all it requires is to take action and do it. Although you may do it wrongly in the beginning, but you'll always want to follow the correct formula. I mean, there's really no point of trying out different formulas when the existing formula has already been proven to work for so many others.

Maybe this text hasn't caused an epiphany for you yet. But for me, I know if I start to send more traffic to a proven seller, focus on just what matters at the moment of time and follow a proven formula, I'm going to make even more money than I'm doing right now.

32. WHAT'S WRONG WITH MY TRAFFIC?

Traffic chasing. Crazed over getting website traffic. How many eBooks have you read or how many courses have you attended that claimed to show you how to get thousands of traffic--or even millions--if you were to follow their teachings exactly?

I have several of those books. In fact, some of them are right. They really do work... except you are only getting "useless" traffic, the type that don't convert to sales.

Focus, Aim, Fire!

You see, it is near pointless getting traffic unless it is targeted traffic. So that same effort to get 10,000 useless visitors is best used to get 100 targeted visitors.

For example, if you have a "scuba diving" website and you are getting traffic from people interested in parrots, you are not going to make any money from them.

What you want is targeted traffic. It doesn't matter even if you get very little traffic of this type-because it will be able to convert to real money for you.

What do I mean by "targeted" traffic?

This traffic is made up of visitors who are looking for you or for the solutions you provide. For instance, if someone found you from the search engines, this is a targeted visitor because he's searching for you indirectly.

The worst type of traffic you want to generate is the "forced" type. For instance, spamming is considered a "forced" traffic strategy simply because the audience or email recipients had never requested the information, but it was sent to them anyway.

What you want to do right now is just to focus on 2 or 3 targeted traffic-generation strategies. Get the right visitors to your website and begin making money first.

Don't try to chase more traffic strategies because there are a thousand and one ways to get traffic. The fastest way to achieve this is to use pay-per-click advertising like Google Adwords or Facebook advertising. You will be able to get targeted traffic instantly if you know how to advertise properly.

Another good strategy is writing and publishing acontent online. If someone visits your website because he found you from reading your article, you can bet that he is very interested in what you do. Also, he has already accepted you as an expert in your niche and this will increase his responsiveness to your sales copy.

Once you start getting targeted visitors to your website, you need to know how to monetize the traffic. Therefore, the next thing to learn is copywriting skills and apply sales conversion strategies to sell your products there. Business is still business whether offline or online. You can't expect to succeed unless you learn how to communicate effectively with other people.

I have been contacted by several businesspeople who told me that their website is getting traffic each month but they are not making money online with it. This was because they were not selling any products that were related to what the visitors were searching for! Sometimes, it was their website that wasn't presented well enough for their visitors to buy.

Don't worry about asking your visitors to buy your stuff. By asking for sales, you will see some sales begin rolling in very soon. Ask for orders! Try it if you don't believe me.

In conclusion, what I am stressing is that the key to success online is getting targeted traffic — not just any old traffic, because it is much easier to monetize targeted traffic with excellent sales copywriting on your webpage.

33. WHY YOUR PRODUCT WON'T MAKE YOU MONEY

Do you really think that simply having your own product to sell online will make you money?

You will be grossly disappointed if you think that is true. It is not about the product whatsoever. Yes, having your own product is a great advantage, but having the asset of your online business will make you money. A lot of money. Keep that in mind: own an asset, not a product if you want to be successful online.

What do I mean?

The asset of your online business is your database, your list. Here is a "big secret" of business success: If you just focus your online business model on building a database of customers and subscribers, you will make money online regardless of whether you have a product of your own or not!

Now, if you were to combine that with niche marketing, you are going to laugh all the way to the bank!

Imagine having a huge database of people interested in "model trains" and no one else is trying to market to them. You will have their full attention each time you recommend a product related to "model trains" for them to buy!

Fewer competitors/marketers, more profits for you.

Why bother learning how to create your own product? What you should focus on is how to make money online! Creating and selling your own product is just one of the many different ways.

Build an asset. Build your own database. Build a mailing list today.

34. CREATING THE "CORRECT" WEBPAGE

If you read carefully, I didn't say, "creating the correct website" but "creating the correct webpage". The idea here is to create a webpage, not a website -- if you want to get results and make money faster.

I know Yahoo.com, Amazon.com and Google.com have all been very successful websites. But, do you know how many people have tried to do that and failed? And don't forget how much time and money those big companies have invested in to achieve it?

Those who failed wasted a lot of time and money there. I am not saying that you shouldn't go and start another Amazon.com. If you want to, please go ahead. However, I am recommending to you an easier and cheaper way to make money from the internet.

If you're selling an info-product, what you want to create is a direct-response webpage like www.wakeupmillionaire.com. A direct-response webpage is good for making money.

A direct-response webpage is one that prompts the visitor to take action, like buying your product, answering a survey, subscribing to your mailing list and so on. The mistake that many people make when doing business on the internet is trying to sell something the first time someone visits their webpage!

Sure, there is always a possibility they might buy on the first visit but the percentage of those who do buy is higher on subsequent visits to your site. The fact is, unless you are faced with compulsive or impulsive shoppers, people usually don't buy the very first time they see a product.

Why?

For the simple reason that most people are just not used to buying a product when they first see it! They may be skeptical and they would prefer to find out more about the product first. Secondly, you don't have a relationship with your new prospect yet.

Would you prefer to buy a product from a friend or a complete stranger?

I bet it would be from a friend or at least someone with whom you have had previous contact.

The mechanism of selling is the same in the internet business as in other types of business. You want to build rapport with your visitors so they will trust you and feel truly comfortable buying from you.

Making It Really Work

Here is the real important part: You must collect your visitors' names and email addresses when they visit your webpage so that you can send them more emails in the future. I absolutely do not recommend you sell to them on their first visit to your webpage. I recommend that you sell to them through emails once you have built rapport with them.

35. AUTOMATE YOUR ONLINE BUSINESS OR ELSE YOU WON'T HAVE A LIFE

Everything's done. Let's say you are making money online now but you are not free. You have to run the online business. If that is the case, you are not successful because you can't enjoy your income to the maximum when you don't have enough time to spend the money.

What you want to do is automate the business as much as possible so you can work less. I will be honest with you: it is impossible to stop working 100 per cent. However, if you can work only 2 to 4 hours a day, that is a great achievement, especially compared to those who have to work 8 a day, and dragging themselves to work every day. Also, you get to pick your own working hours and location!

There are a few tasks in your online business that you can automate, or should I say, you must automate.

1. Your *payment collection*: Use a credit card system that can take payment and automatically send customers the products they ordered. You don't want to take orders manually. Trust me.

2. *Email*: *You must* use an autoresponder to follow up with your subscribers or customers. You will go crazy if you have to manually send emails to them. It is impossible to do this when you have hundreds of people in your database. I use www.sendaweber.com.

3. *Affiliate system:* If you want others to help you sell your product, you must have a good affiliate tracking system in place. Not only will you be fooling yourself thinking that you can track it manually, no affiliates will promote your product if they are not confident that their efforts will be duly rewarded. A proper system includes creating a duplicate website of yours for your affiliates, stats tracking, and accurate commission payment. I use www.clickbank.com and for Malaysia, I use www.affiliates.com.my

With at least three of these "backroom" processes out of the way, you can now focus on bringing in more sales and expanding your business -- and yes, have a life too.

36. HOW TO GET THEM TO BUY

We base a lot of assumptions on why a visitor will buy our product. Most of the time, we assume that we have a superior product. But truthfully, all product creators and authors have this weakness.

Have you really asked yourself: "What do my web visitors need to know before they will buy from me?"

A prospect needs to know two things before he or she will buy from you. First, "Does your product or service solve my problem?" Obviously, the answer should always be "yes".

So this leads to a new challenge, the second thing: What do you have to convince them that your product will actually solve their problem? No, not because your sales letter says so, but why they should literally trust you!

Your words can make people pull out their wallets and be ecstatic about receiving a mediocre product if you know the secrets behind copywriting. Knowing how to use the power of words to make people not only pay you money but do almost whatever you desire is downright frightening!

So use this skill carefully and ethically.

The best way is to use testimonials. Try to get these from your past customers instead of your own "cronies" that you have paid. Other than that...

Show them your *results!*

If you are selling a "how to lose weight" product, show the "before" and "after" images. It's easy. Take a picture of yourself before use and take another after you have lost some weight.

If you're selling a product on how to grow hair, do exactly the same. Take the "before" and "after" pictures.

If you are selling a course teaching people how to make money online, then show them the income you have earned from the internet.

Show them proof, that is what I am saying.

Most people don't want to buy first before seeing others getting results because they are afraid of making a mistake. As soon as one or two people have bought your product and have benefited from the results, you will get a flock of sales. It is like a "follow the leader" kind of game. It is an amazing spectacle of crowd psychology in action.

The next question that pops up in your visitor's mind is probably, "Can I trust you to deliver the solution that you promised?"

Most websites violate both of these rules and unnecessarily limit their sales by doing so. You can now play the game much more successfully and make a lot more sales for each unique that comes visitor to your site.

To apply these rules ask yourself this question: "Does my website's design and copy inspire trust and *confidence*?"

Look at every single element of your site with this question in your mind.

You probably have heard of the saying, "Too much of something is not good." However, too many testimonials can *never be bad*! So if you can add a lot of supportive evidence to your claims, add them.

You will find that your webpage will now take on a completely different "look" and you will automatically know what else needs to be changed. If necessary, you should have someone else look at your webpage and ask them the question, "If you didn't know it was my site, would you buy anything from this website?"

Get their honest reaction.

All that a new visitor to your site has to go on with are your graphics and words. People are very skeptical and they discount (distrust) 90 per cent of what you say. Give them a reason to believe you. Include your address and phone number on your webpage if it's necessary. Do what you can to assure them that they have a reason to trust you.

Don't forget that 98 per cent of all human beings buy products or services emotionally and then justify those purchases logically afterwards. Change the things you need to change, add proof, add testimonials, and add anything else that will back-up your claims and ease the mind of the potential customer -- including a strong "risk reversal" money-back guarantee. You will start making more sales. This is my guarantee.

37. WANNA BE AN ONLINE ENTREPRENEUR?

Me! Me! Me!

That is what I hear from the crowd -- the dream of becoming an online entrepreneur.

Yes, you can~! But you need to know eight of these success principles first:

1.   Say "No" To Ridiculous Sales Letters

If you have been reading sales letters, you know what kinds of hype other people are trying to sell you. Forget about "Getting Rich Quick!" whenever you read one.

If you are looking to "get rich quick", you better take some heavy risks or be super lucky, because in the world of internet business, just like any other business, it takes both time and hard work. There is no way around it. But there are sure ways to make it simpler and quicker.

2.   Stop Looking For The "Secret" to Internet Success

Here it is: There is no secret that the online marketers making the most profits have the largest lists. Of course, when I say "large list", I mean a large list of people who are *responsive*.

The quickest way to build your list and keep in constant contact with your prospects is to start building one. I told you, it's no secret of mine. If you don't believe me, go on and buy more courses to seek the "true" secret to internet success.

3.   Freebies Work Fine For Marketing

Freebies are the best way to generate leads and build your list. Free reports, free eBooks, free software... use any or all of these to gather new email addresses and your list will build in no time. In exchange for those freebies, your visitors are going to leave their names and email addresses for you to contact them.

This strategy is very effective, especially if you are not in the super competitive market of the "internet marketing" niche. Unless you are a big kahuna in the internet marketing scene, then this method will work extremely well for you. For instance, any speaker featured in The Secret and talks about *Law Of Attraction* (LOA) will naturally sell very well, regardless of whether their talk is valuable or not. But someone who knows everything about LOA won't have a single audience if he is not "branded".

4. Find Your Niche And You Will Find Your Riches

You have heard it over a million times: You need a niche market. End of story. Build a website geared around your niche and you can start developing all kinds of online revenue. Up sell, down sell, cross sell, whatever sell, you name it.

5. Boring But Important To Have These

Patience and focused tenacity are both key, my friend. It took me 3 years to be where I am today and I don't consider myself to be doing anything great yet. There is more to come and I believe I will go leaps and bounds as long as I have... patience and focused tenacity.

6. How Committed Are You To Being An Online Entrepreneur?

Can you make a simple commitment to send emails to at least 3 joint venture partners to promote your product on a daily basis? There are two major reasons for doing this. *Momentum* is a key factor in keeping you dedicated to your online goal of entrepreneurship, and numbers is the game for getting JVs when you start--heck, even when you are a seasoned marketer it still applies.

If you are already starting to whine and groan over this advice, then forget about living your online entrepreneur dream.

7. Spending Your Time At The Right Place

The majority of your time should be spent on marketing. That's it. It's nothing surprising, but many "entrepreneurs" waste a lot of their time trying to work with the 90 per cent who aren't going to put money into their pocket.

8. Going To The Next Level

Once you have made some money online, don't go and buy that sports car or expensive toy you have been dreaming of. Instead, *invest in you*--in your own education and tools that can enhance both your mind and your business. That is what a true online entrepreneur will do, even though it does not seem glamorous at first.

Till then, stay focus on what you want to achieve.

38. 3 WAYS OF INCREASING YOUR AFFILIATE COMMISSIONS

If you're a newbie and not sure what an affiliate program is, here's what it is in a nutshell...

Affiliate programs (also called Referral Programs or Partnership Programs) are essentially commission-based sales schemes. You recommend a site to your website visitors and pick up a given percentage of any sales that those visitors generate. This percentage of sales is considered as an affiliate commission. You benefit from the commission and the site benefits from the sales it wouldn't otherwise have made if it wasn't for you, as an affiliate marketer.

Here are 3 ways to increase your affiliate commission:

1.   Offer Time-Limited or Number-Limited Bonuses

You probably already know that one quick and easy way to beat your competing affiliates is to add value to the products and services you promote.

So while your affiliates are just promoting the offer as-is, you're giving your customers a valuable freebie if they choose to buy from you.

For example, let's suppose you're selling a diet book. You can offer a free diet recipe book to anyone who buys directly from your link. And you can bet more people will buy from your link simply because they get more bang for their buck.

To make this tactic even more powerful, you can offer a "limited" amount of bonuses. For instance, the bonuses will only be given to only the first X number of people who act now to buy.

2.   Write Case Studies Showing How You've Achieved Results

Using the Product

People are looking for social proof.

They want to see that other people have used and enjoyed the product.

But here's the thing – most of the social proof your prospects see is absolutely lame. They'll see a review for a diet book that says, "Fast read! I love this stuff!" They'll excitedly read one affiliate's opinion on an affiliate marketing book only to find it says, "*WOW! This is truly amazing! I know I'll make a gazillion dollars with these tips!*"

Your prospects are not looking for theory. Instead – they are looking for real proof that the product/service does exactly what it's advertised to do.

That's where your case study comes in.

Instead of just writing a review, you use the product and report your results. And you back up your case study with other forms of proof whenever possible, such as before and after pictures, videos, screenshots, etc. Anything that can help to prove your claims.

3.   Develop Your Own Ads and Content

Think about this from your customers' perspective.

If they are on a lot of mailing lists, and/or if they're doing some product research, they're bound to run into many different affiliates who are all promoting the same product.

Problem is, they're going to run into the same ads over and over again. And if they're on multiple mailing lists, they're going to get the exact same email repeatedly.

Eventually they're going to develop ad blindness for all these similar ads. And when the prospect sees that same email coming into their inbox, they'll delete it.

If you use the same ads and content as everyone else – AND if you're not one of the first your prospect encounters – they won't be buying from you, simple.

That's why you need to develop your own ads and content to promote the affiliate program.

Now here's the best part –

Combine three of them in your affiliate program. It'll skyrocket your commission.

Note: If you're new to affiliate marketing and need a complete A-Z training, you should head to **www.patricchan.net/affiliatemarketing.**

39. WHY I STOPPED OFFLINE ADVERTISING

The key to making lots of money is to keep costs low, and profits high. That is the exact reason why I market info-products entirely online. Digital products are low cost and advertising online is relatively cheap compared to offline marketing. Let me give you a brief example.

I used to run advertisements in local newspapers to advertise my internet marketing workshop. It is an ad announcing a free 2-hour seminar which I conduct, and at the end of the seminar I would sell a $2,000 workshop to those interested. The free seminar was a sort of preview, but it was content-packed to give value.

Now, this ad will would cost me $2,000 regardless of whether there are people seeing it or not. Understand this -- the circulation of the newspaper does not determine how many readers actually see my advertisement.

From it, we might get 80 people calling up our office to confirm attending this free 2-hour seminar. So in a nutshell, we will generate 80 interested participants at the cost of $25 ($2,000/80) per inquiry.

But we might end up getting only 50 participants who actually turn up. This meant it cost us a whopping $40 ($2,000/50 free seminar participants) per lead!

Wasn't that crazy?

Well, it depends on how you look at it. If you are making money, then it isn't crazy. But one thing is for sure, marketing offline can be really costly. Costly means risky, because money is just flowing out from your pocket if not done correctly.

This is where I will introduce to you how marketing online can be ridiculously cheap when compared to offline advertising.

Behold, the power of Adwords at www.google.com/adwords!

As mentioned in earlier chapters, I am not going to explain how it works because you can simply find the details at www.google.com/adwords. But what I want you to realize is this: you have the *opportunity to compete with multi-million-dollar businesses at a very low cost!*

For instance, getting an ad of yours clicked online is just like getting a phone inquiry in the offline world.

How much will it cost you? Maximum of a buck, a dollar. And that is on the high range. I will probably spend less than $0.50 for a click. But in the offline advertising example earlier, I had to spend $25 for a single "click"!

When I saw the potential of this, I gave up on advertising in the offline world... *unless* I absolutely have to, which is really, really rare these days.

Then there is another issue with offline advertising: you can't know how many people *actually* see your print or broadcast advertisement. However, when you are marketing online, you can calculate all of the varying metrics and have the statistics at your fingertips.

For Adwords advertising in particular, you can see how many times your ad is exposed to a website visitor, how many times it has being clicked on, as well as other cool metrics.

What does this tell you?

Marketing online can be tracked and tested easily. So we aren't talking about guessing games but scientific methods to advertise your business at a very low cost here.

To get the best results from your Adwords marketing campaigns is easy because there are only three main components to focus on. There are more than that of course, but these are the *main ones.*

1.   The Keywords

What are the best keywords to use? Although this is subjective, a simple guideline is to have specific but smart *keywords.* Like, if your business is about "parenting", don't go and use the keyword "parenting". Use keywords like "parenting advice", "how to teach a child", etc.

2.   Your Ad
You have three short lines to describe your ad to "sell" the call-to-action. So don't waste it. Write it as specific as you can and use benefit-orientated

sentences. If you have any unique selling points like "today", "instantly", "free", etc. don't save them--use them like there is *no tomorrow.*

3.   Your Landing Page

Where does your ad lead the visitor to? Your site. No, I don't to write that to be sarcastic. There are advertisers who lead their visitors to an affiliate program they are promoting to make a quick buck. That is their choice of course, but my personal preference is sending visitors to my own site first. This not only enables me to turn the visitors into subscribers first before sending them away to a sales page, but it also allows me to control my pre-sell -- selling to them before they see the sales pitch which will "pre-frame" or prime their mind to buy in advance.

It is important to have a landing page that *matches your ad's* description closely to get a higher conversion rate and lower your bid price.

The real "gold" to this whole thing is the ability for you to test and track. Simple tweaks to your keywords, ads and the landing pages can result in huge profit increases to your business. And I don't mean just about your online business -- you can always use this tool to promote your offline business anywhere in the world, presuming there are surfers looking for it online.

Any final advice?

Yes. Don't get your brain messed up by running too many campaigns.

Manage one campaign properly before considering going into another niche. This goes back to the basic 101 marketing fundamentals of understanding your market first.

Note: Google Adwords is very powerful, however, it's rather strict in approving ads. The alternative is using Facebook Advertising.

40. THE SECRET OF CREATING MONEY ON DEMAND

I have demonstrated making money online on demand in front of live audiences of hundreds in a seminar room previously, back in 2005 and again in 2006. Many of the participants were purely amazed -- not that I made a lot of money, but the fact that money could be created seemingly out of "thin air" from the internet.

Just like they did, you are probably going to ask me this: "What is your secret, Patric?"

Well, I should say I have a *secret formula* so that I can feel absolutely intelligent and sagely.

But darn, being a really nice guy, I am compelled to tell you the truth... and that the only "secret" to successful internet marketing is this -- there are no secrets.

The very use of the word "secret" is a marketing tactic and I too am guilty of using it occasionally. Is it wrong to do so? Is there something wrong with marketing tactics? Marketing is not wrong... just somewhat creative.

The fact remains that internet marketing still involves work and lots of it. When I say I know a lot of successful internet marketing gurus, I am not bragging. But to lead-in to another truth--these people work really hard. Some work like a dog. Personally, I think I work like a dog, sometimes... of course, in a positive way.

I know many will dislike me telling this truth. It just shattered the dreams of many people who think that internet business is the path to easy financial freedom and to stop working. In a way, this is good because it will get rid of those who don't have an enterprising and hardworking spirit.

In fact, it has been my experience that internet marketing is not a quick and easy path to "easy money". But if you are planning to build a real business, I think it is much easier doing it online than setting up your own brick-and-mortar shop in your hometown, whether in the retail, food or service business.

Generating a sustainable income via internet marketing does not happen overnight. Success is fleeting, especially early on, until you establish yourself in your niche market and then slowly begin to dominate it.

Internet marketing takes a lot of hard work, persistence, knowledge, creativity, and above all else, time. It is not the quick and easy road to riches that some would have you believe.

Internet marketing also has a very high learning curve because you need to learn marketing, business and a few of the technical aspects. In a nutshell, it takes both time and effort to master.

I have been involved with internet marketing for 7 years now and have experienced some major successes of my own. But even then, I am still learning all the time.

Now, if you are marketing in the internet marketing niche itself, expect to double your effort and time because you will be competing with giants and legends like Eben Pagan, Frank Kern, Shawn Casey, Anik Singal, Mike Filsaime, Russell Brunson, Stephen Pierce, Ewen Chia, Yanik Silver, Ryan Deiss, Andrew Fox, Jim Edwards, Chris Carpenter, Alex Jeffreys, Armand Morin, John Chow, Adam Ginsberg, Matt Bacak, Gary Ambrose, Jeff Walker, Jo Han Mok, Alex Mandossian, Jeremy Gislason, Peng Joon and gosh ... who else did I miss? Ah, yes, also with Patric Chan (Truthfully, I can easily name an extra 100 names of successful marketers to the list above.)

"Patric, you're supposed to say how great internet marketing is!"

Yes, it is great, *unfathomably* great! However, if I don't reveal what really happens behind the scenes, I am doing you a great disservice, and to some extent, creating false hope for good people like you and others.

It is simple. If what I have said did not scare or turn you off, then you are probably going to be one of those true success cases with internet marketing. Your name will be widely known in your niche. You know what your obstacles are and you will be able to overcome them with a click of your fingers.

Although it isn't easy, it is worth doing it. Just imagine -- the ability to execute "money on demand". Now, that is an inspiration that will take you far.

If I hadn't started 11 years ago, I don't think I would be able to make money as easily as I want today. Yes, I do everything from a click of a button.

I don't care that it had taken me years to achieve this because it was all worth it -- every single drop of sweat from those years. This is because creating wealth was never this easy in my life, especially for someone who never attended college or university and who does not write fluently in English.

Remember now, I have already said that there are no secrets unless the secret to internet marketing success is a mixture of hard work, dedication, perseverance, patience, creativity, time, knowledge, etc.

Of course this isn't a secret that would sell very well now, is it?

Try going out and tell obese people that they need to stop eating junk food and wake up at 6:30 AM to exercise for an hour every day. I think that kind of advice would definitely not sell even though it is the right advice.

No one wants to hear something like that for free, much less do they want to pay to hear something like that! But I guess if no one wants to be the "bad" guy, I will take that responsibility of revealing the truth.

There is *no* secret ... but there is a sure-fire method to achieve success online. This method can help you to generate money on demand. And it is...

Having A Mailing List!

No, not just some stupid unfocused mailing list so you can blast your promotion everywhere. (Anyone can get that from a phonebook directory!) I am talking about a list of real people who read your emails regularly and take action because they like and trust you.

I can guess your next question will be: "How do I build a mailing list, Patric?"

Simple. Go and reread some of the earlier chapters! Yes, please do precisely that. Well, since we're here, I am going to do a quick "refresher course" here.

Make sure all of your websites have an opt-in mechanism that visitors can use to subscribe to your list. So if this answer applies to you, your main focus is to drive *traffic* to your site. That's it!

I mean, come on -- you can't build a list if you don't have any traffic. And as I mentioned in earlier chapters, you can create traffic by using social media, PPC, viral marketing, blogging, etc. Ironically, the "secret" is not about building a mailing list either! I am not trying to be philosophical or make you downright confused ... I am trying to paint a bigger picture in your brain. It is about knowing how to *build a relationship and apply permission marketing* to your list.

The simplest advice I can give you on this is: If your subscribers were your friends, what would you email to them periodically to make sure that they gain value from you? Answer that correctly and you will have a good list, a money-making cash cow, if you like.

Success is there for the taking, friends, if you make up your mind from the beginning to see where you can be.

Despite the claims of "easy money" being made by thousands of internet gurus the world over, you *will* have to work hard and persevere. You can't do "nothing" and watch the cash roll into your PayPal account. It just doesn't work that way, friends. But it sure works if you start planting your seeds today. Yes, right now. You see, success doesn't happen overnight but in small increments. If you are serious about building a successful online business, no one can make it happen other than you yourself.

Once you are there, I hope to receive an email from you saying, "Patric, I took your advice and I am successful today."

Note: If you want to join my coaching program for list marketing, please go to **www.patricchan.net/coaching**

41. FIVE PIECE OF "COMMON SENSE" ADVICE

1. **You need money, not a lot but enough money to do internet marketing.** Ironically, the money is best spend on acquiring knowledge. And sometimes, you "over-spend" because you ended up learning from the wrong "Gurus" and they took your money away.

I know, it's a "chicken and egg story" – people go online because they don't have money and wanted to make money there, right? And this is also the reason how unethical marketers are able to use the Internet to find their victims. When someone is in desperation, they WANT to believe in false promises, even when they sound so unreal. It's sad, but that's the truth.

2. **Need to invest in time.** It took someone years to be good at his job and get paid well, what makes him feel that he can master internet marketing in just weeks, or even months? Internet marketing is a "business skill" – not everyone is crafted to be enterprising, so you need to accept that it'll take some time to immerse this skill.

3. **Do things quick, be adaptive.** Remember the internet marketing course (or eBook) you bought 6 months ago and haven't opened it yet? Well, if it's about a particular tactic on how to make money online, I would guess that it's no longer as effective as it claims to be anymore. Heck, it might not even work anymore whatsoever. My advice? Start doing it now – don't wait and complain later.

4. **You're not the only dude.** You might think that you have an awesome idea or product. Now, that could be true but at the same time, MANY people out there have awesome ideas and products too. Just take the lucrative internet marketing niche as an example – there are thousands of courses today with many self-proclaimed internet marketing gurus. Your only "differentiation" is most likely the marketing strategies that you have. By the way, don't get confused that internet marketing gurus are marketing geniuses – most of them are not, they simply have bigger lists

and a lot of "friends" to promote for them. Really, it's nothing further than that.

5. Stick to one. I can't even remember how many times I've wrote about this – you need to focus on just one opportunity at a time. Multiple streams of income don't really work if you can't get one of those income streams to stabilize. And I'm not just referring to income streams, this apply to almost everything – In the past, I used to be a big fan of article marketing, but today, I've stopped doing article marketing even though it's fully automated (I have writers and software to submit). You may ask why... the answer is this – less things to think and care about, and more "space" for other things to do.

Here's an additional piece of advice...

6. Money will always be there. You see, as long as you work hard (and smart, of course) to master internet marketing, there will always be money to be made from the Internet. Here's something I would like to share with you, from the CEO of Coca Cola, Bryan Dyson:

"Imagine life as a game in which you are juggling some five balls in the air. You name them – Work, Family, Health, Friends and Spirit and you're keeping all of these in the Air.

You will soon understand that work is a rubber ball. If you drop it, it will bounce back.

But the other four Balls – Family, Health, Friends and Spirit – are made of glass. If you drop one of these; they will be irrevocably scuffed, marked, nicked, damaged or even shattered. They will never be the same. You must understand that and strive for it."

42. IT'S THE QUALITY THAT MATTERS, NOT QUANTITY

I don't know how many affiliates you have in your affiliate program that will promote your product. I have over 1,000 registered affiliates, but I think there are only 5 per cent that bring results to the table.

Just in case you have forgotten what affiliates are, they are the resellers whom you pay a certain commission for promoting your products on the internet.

Coming back to our lesson, you are probably asking why are 95 per cent of the affiliates are not doing anything. I don't know, but I am sure they have good reasons for not wanting to earn any commissions from me.

But I don't let this bother me -- neither should you. You do what you are capable of doing, like providing the marketing tools or training to everyone you can. Remember, what you are *capable of.* That's it. We can't arm-twist others to help make us rich.

But, you communicate with the performers, in my case, those in my 5 per cent group. Send a personal email to your affiliates who have made past sales for you. Build a relationship with them. They will end up preferring to promote your products over others after they get to know you as an individual.

You have to accept the fact that you can't help everyone even if you want to. For affiliates who don't know how to promote as an affiliate, guide them if you can, but don't squander your time there if you think they are taking up your time. You might as well use your time to communicate with the real performers who bring you results. As for those non-performers whom you think are genuine, I would strongly suggest that you recommend them to a good resource to learn about affiliate marketing.

The Next Step

Once you are earning a lot of income from your top affiliates, what do you do next?

Ask them what else you can do to help them to make more money for you and them! (By then you should have so much rapport with them that frank discussions are easy.)

Now once they no longer need your attention that much anymore, you can focus on the 95 per cent of the under-performing affiliates.

Does that sound ruthless? I hope not, because you are either running a business or a charity, and you need to decide which. Focus on making money from your business first -- and then you can do charity with the money made!

Your only "differentiation" is most likely the marketing strategies that you have. By the way, don't get confused that internet marketing gurus are marketing geniuses – most of them are not, they simply have bigger lists and a lot of "friends" to promote for them.

43. WHY ARE YOU PROMOTING SOMEONE ELSE'S PRODUCT AS AN AFFILIATE?

To earn affiliate commission?

That is true ... but there is another important reason that must come first, and before thinking about yourself making a profit.

Yes, you want to help your subscribers or visitors. Only then, will you want to make your affiliate commission.

Does this sound corny or cheesy?

Sure. But don't you think that is the wiser thing to do? If you recommend a product and the customer is happy after buying it, you are going to get more business from them. It's just logical and practical. Besides that, you will feel happier when you go to sleep at night.

If you start to change your thoughts and focus on how to add value to other people's lives by becoming an affiliate, rather than thinking about how to make money, you will get excited about it and become more prosperous, believe me. You will cut down stress levels because you are not desperate for sales anymore.

"Okay, I'm sold! So how do I choose what products to promote, Patric?"

Whatever products you plan to promote for commissions, you *must like them, or have reviewed them first.* There is no exception to this rule.

Imagine if you have never been to Hawaii, can you truly recommend that your friends go there for a holiday? But if you had been there and enjoyed it, I guess you would be all excited to tell your friends about the place.

In my experience, I have never promoted a product that I haven't reviewed personally unless it is a product that somehow cannot be reviewed, like a teleseminar or a product or service that hasn't been created yet. Even if I did, I will make sure that I know the creator or organizer personally so that I can rest assured that he will deliver exactly what he claims.

There are many reasons why you need to do that. However, I think the main reason is, you don't want to associate your name with rotten apples. If you promote a product blindly, do you think your subscribers or visitors will trust you again if the products they bought through you were not up to the claims substantiated?

Maybe. But if you did that five times, *you are out!*

"But if I followed your advice, Patric, I won't have time to review all of the products that I want to promote."

So, don't promote them!

For instance, I get quite a number of JV proposals each week. Sometimes, I will just politely turn some down because I just don't have the time to review them.

It's okay. Don't worry about losing the affiliate commission. Plan and think ahead long term. You might make a lot of money right now but over time, people will start to lose their trust in you if you keep on promoting products that you simply don't know the quality of.

Here is another tip to select a product to promote: Don't promote a similar-function product.

I always try not to promote "similar" products. For instance, I won't promote three types of autoresponder to my prospects to choose from. I will just promote one, the autoresponder that I use. Why? Because I know this autoresponder is good and reliable.

If you promote more than one product of a similar type, you might get your prospects confused. Just choose one that you think or believe is the absolute best.

Once in a while, you will see a high-end product being promoted online, or it could be a "Fire Sale" promotion. Now, unless you are a pro and have experience with these things, avoid promoting it altogether. Don't get involved with it no matter how big the affiliate commission is. The main reason is that you will be wasting your time, effort and money. But worst of all, you will be disappointed.

Does this sound cold? Good. I like to be frank so that I can teach you something this important.

Recently, I came across an internet marketing seminar that cost $2,997 (or maybe $3,997--I can't remember the price exactly). One of the affiliates to this program was a well-known internet marketing company. If you are not a big-time, experienced player, you wouldn't want to compete with them because they have over 50 valuable products. I think I saw that they were offering bonuses worth over $10,000 if anyone signs up for to the seminar from using their affiliate link.

Now, let's consider this. Do you think someone would rather buy from you, or from this affiliate who is giving away bonuses worth over $10,000?

Secondly, by the time you promoted it, your potential customers might have already bought it from someone else because those same customers are probably subscribed to other mailing lists or visited other websites that are promoting the same product.

My advice? Always choose a great product to promote, but make sure it is not over-exposed.

44. RE: WHAT I LEARN FROM MICROSOFT'S BUSINESS MODEL

Do you know what an Xbox 360 is?

That's a Microsoft's video game console - if you know PlayStation from Sony, Xbox 360 is its competitor.

Of course, they would have the Xbox One now, but the reason I'm talking about its earlier version is because of a business lesson I've learned from it.

Just do a search on the internet for "Xbox 360 red ring" or "Xbox 360 red light problem" and you'll see *millions* of searches. It's so famous that there's even a page on Wikipedia dedicated about it!

See http://en.wikipedia.org/wiki/Xbox_360_technical_problems and there are even info-products about it in clickbank.com previously.

And yet Microsoft is *still selling* its game console despite knowing about this problem (however they might have solved it by now).

Imagine this - when they launch, they sold millions of copies and gotten the feedbacks about the problem but they still keep on selling it.

THEY DON'T STOP SELLING DESPITE KNOWING THE PROBLEM.

Honestly, if I sell a million copy of a product that has problems, I would be majorly stressed. Wouldn't you?

Three business philosophies I've learned from Microsoft's business thinking:

1. You can't wait for everything to be perfect. First, perfection will

probably never exist. By the time you get it 'perfect', whatever you're selling might even be already outdated.

Secondly, you have to be fast if you want to be the market leader. Their competitor, PlayStation was already the market leader at the time and if they didn't act fast, the harder it'll be for them to penetrate in the market. Besides, the longer they waited the more profit they would lose.

2. If you have sales, everything else can be handled. Got a problem after making a lot of sales? Then invest your profit in customer service. The secret to business success - create positive cash flow and reinvest it in your business.
3.
4. The money is in the back-end. Do you think Microsoft just make money from selling the game console? I'm sure you're smarter than that. :-) The games, my friend. *BIG BUCKS.*

I'm not a game developer so I don't know how much game companies pay for the license to have their game playable with Xbox 360. I have no clue whether it's $100 or $10,000, but there are thousands of games developed all the time. But what if Microsoft takes royalty for each game sold? Some games launch with millions of copies sold overnight – do the math and you'll see that Microsoft makes millions of dollars on passive income.

Let's look at your current business now...

Are you launching your internet business even if it's not perfect?

Are you focusing solely on sales, the lifeblood of your business, or something redundant?

And finally, do you have a back-end offer for your existing products?

There are risks involved in businesses. But with a planned business strategy, risks are nothing compared to the return of investment. The point? Don't sweat over your business risk – instead, focus on your business strategy because that's where the reward is.

45. HOW TO RESEARCH FOR A PROFITABLE NICHE MARKET

I'm going to talk about choosing a niche market today.

Well, I guess the most common internet marketing question asked is probably this...

"Tell me, what is the hottest niche market?"

Now, before I jump to the answer, a "good" sustainable niche market should have these elements...

1. It's an evergreen topic where you're not dependent on what's hot today.

2. They are solution/problem-oriented niche markets.

3. There are a lot of sub-topics in one niche. For instance, relationship is an ideal example -- there are so many "categories" of relationship, ranging from dating to sex.

Of course there are many other elements to decide whether a market is good or not, but those listed above are the main ones.

You'll also need to understand that almost any niche market can be profitable as long as you know how to reach them online and have great offers available for them to buy.

To answer your question, these are the hot niches...

1. Self improvement
2. Relationship
3. Health

4. Internet marketing
5. Business opportunities

Notice that all of these markets have the elements above and on top of that, they're "never-ending" topics.

I mean...

People don't stop to improve themselves.

People always want to have a better relationship or intimacy.

Everybody wants to look better and become healthier.

Those involve with internet marketing always want to learn the latest strategies.

Everyone wants to make more money. :)

46. MY 5 MARKETING "WORDS OF WISDOM"

I would like to share my tips for attaining more success with internet marketing and online businesses.

Here are 5 marketing words of wisdom:

1. **Be Innovative (Or Perish)** – It's actually easy to make lots of money online, especially in the internet marketing niche. Here are two mistakes that newbies make when they try to penetrate the internet marketing niche:

   i. They come up with another "old" product idea, for example a course teaching about product creation or blogging. Those are nothing new at all and there are plenty of similar courses out there.

   ii. They are being creative. There's nothing wrong with being creative but don't expect to be a trend setter if you're a newbie without strong influence in the marketplace. Secondly, if it's too new, people might not "get it" or be ready to test it out.

Be innovative. Just see what ideas have been successful and improve upon them. In fact, you can just spot them in Clickbank.com directly; it's really a no-brainer.

2. **Know less, do more.** Most people are unaware of this, but I've been exploring the domain name opportunity for the past several months. In fact, until now, it's still a new game for me. But here's the thing – the more I know, the 'harder' it seems to make money with domains because I'm so overwhelmed with resources and options. THERE ARE A LOT OF THINGS TO LEARN ABOUT DOMAINS. Here's the interesting part – I've started selling domains successfully even though I'm not doing anything fancy. It's as simple as putting it in Sedo.com. Once sold, I just buy more domains. The point is, sometimes you just need to *know less* and *do more* of what you already know how to do.

3. **Need A Team.** After spending about 18 months with Robert Allen, I've learned a lot of lessons on success from him, directly and indirectly. One of the things I've noticed about Robert is that he is a master of creating a "dream" team. Be willing to share your piece of cake and you'll get a good team to work with you. If you want to know the 5 other million-dollar lessons I've learned from Bob, you can watch it on Youtube for free, http://youtu.be/J6UCnFZ3DMI

4. **Asian Market.** the past 12 months, I've seen an encouraging rise of customers and clients from the Asian market – in my *online* product sales. It doesn't matter if you're an Asian or a Caucasian, I suggest that you do not leave out the Asian market, especially in years to come. I'm predicting that it's going to boom, and get much bigger. China would be hard to penetrate because it's an eco-system of its own, but there's a huge market for Singapore and Malaysia. With Japan, you probably need your stuff to be in Japanese.

5. **Take A Risk.** I've taught thousands of people to make money online and to start internet businesses. I'm not saying this to be egotistical but to lead to this simple fact – *most people who achieved success are willing to take risks.* For instance, risk of losing other things (mainly time and money).

Take the iconic leader, Steve Jobs – his salary as the CEO of Apple was only $1. Do you think he's going to achieve success with Apple when his bank account is going to depend solely on his performance? Now, that's "risky". But then, that's what leaders do – they take risks so that their reward in is gigantic.

I hope some of these "word of wisdom" will help you be successful this year. Regardless, it is my sincere wish that you'll experience greater success next year and in years to come.

I'm looking forward to growing with you, and reaching the next level.

47. MPS

How was last year?

Did you achieve your internet business goal?

If not, no more messing around – you're set to start an internet business and make money online.

There are 3 things you need to master if you truly want to achieve success on the internet:, M-P-S:

1. (M) Mindset

Honestly, I think most people in the world don't get this, especially those in the internet marketing world. They think mindset is just some hocus-pocus, positive thinking stuff. Yeah, there are some internet marketers out there who become rich without reading personal improvement books, listening to success audios, or attending seminars – but they DO HAVE THE SUCCESS MINDSET. Don't you think mastering persistency, overcoming procrastination, creating self-confidence and so on are related to success mindset? Put it this way, having the desire to achieve success or to become successful IS related to mindset.

2. (P) Platform

You can be all fired up to achieve success but that's not going to happen if you don't know or don't have the vehicle. I learned from Robert Allen that there 4 great vehicles you can use – real estate, stocks, internet, and business. My pick is the Internet (and I guess you're the same too). Make sure you immerse yourself and know as much as you can about internet marketing.

3. (S) Strategy

Choosing and knowing what platform you want to use will make you become like one of the many millions of people out there. Now you need Strategy. Strategy is about having a step-by-step plan and knowing how to execute the steps that will lead you to achieve success online. Where do you get a Strategy? Easy. From people who have already achieved success – it could be from the books, audios, seminars, etc. of these people or simply from knowing them as friends. Especially in our Internet Marketing world, there are countless of courses out there to teach you the Strategy.

That leads me to another question - what else can you do to ensure success? You have to determine this for next year:

Who Are You Learning From?

Let's be honest – there are hundreds of "gurus" and teachers out there who are teaching about making money online. Heck, "gurus" who hardly make any money online are doing that to make money too! So who are you learning from? If your answer is everyone, then I suggest you review your progress so far.

What Is Your Sub-Platform

I talked about choosing your platform earlier. Right now, you have to decide what sub-platform you're going to use to make money online. There are many ways. You can make money online with eBay, internet marketing affiliate programs, Adsense, blogging, Clickbank, niche products, Amazon, niche marketing, eBooks, website flipping, CPA and so on. Once you know that, then it's easy for you to plan out the steps to get there and of course, to select the right mentor to guide you.

Are You Removing All Of The Noise

Every day, there will be a new idea or software to make money online. They'll look awesome and perhaps, they are awesome. The problem is that you won't be able to implement all of them. The best way to stay focused is NOT to know about them. I know, it sounds like an extreme move and you might be worried that you're missing out on something good by not staying updated. Trust me, if it's really that good, you'll hear about it somehow. YOU NEED TO BE VERY FOCUSED.

48. HOW TO TURN A FREE EBOOK INTO A QUALITY $197 PRODUCT

Let's say you have this free eBook that's of good quality, around 100 pages. Here's how to take it and turn it into a $197 information product:

First, increase the perceived value.

Free information is perceived to have a low value, especially free blog posts.

For instance, eBooks have a perceived value of $7 to $28.

Mp3 audio products are generally perceived at around $47.

Downloadable videos can be perceived up to $97 a piece.

Software is perceived anywhere between $97 to the $1,000s.

These are estimates based on studying marketing and observing prices. Some might disagree but that's okay.

Turn your eBook into a form of downloadable media with higher perceived value by doing it yourself or hiring someone to do it cheaply at Elance.com.

If you want to do a screen captured video, use Camtasia or a cheaper program like it.

Then, add the right packaging to increase perceived value even more.

Let's say you took your free eBook and turned it into a 4-hour screen capture instructional video course. Now you're selling it for $97. If you offer 50% commissions to affiliates, you can have a ton of Super Affiliates promoting the quality product that has high value and high perceived value for $43.50 per commission.

What if I told you that by making two minor adjustments you could triple the cost of this product and it'll still have value?

Here's what you can do...

1) Call it a "course.".

2) Go to your graphics guy and tell him, "Instead of creating a graphic for just one 4-hour-video, make it look like 4 DVD's in a bulk package."

Now you have a bulk package that you could sell for $ 97 or more. If it's a course in bulk, the perception will be that your product is an investment.

Before you can get your customer to want to buy your product, you need to give them another big reason why.

You need to make it look like your product's price is a drop in the bucket compared to the benefits that the prospect customer will get!

So we do two things:

1) Pile on quality bonuses like audios, reports, interviews, you name it. This increases value.

2) You need a USP, a Unique Selling Proposition. You'll need something of high perceived and unique value to close the deal. In your case, you could offer mentoring, a free critique, or free coaching of some kind.

These two things significantly increase the perceived value as well as the actual value of your product, which is now a service as well. A costumer passionate about your subject would be willing to invest $197 as a one-time fee for $1,000s of dollars' worth of products and services on your topic.

The great news is that anyone can do this with a how-to eBook.

So that's how you go from giving away a free eBook to making an easy $197 or more on the internet (and that's just 100 visitors to your sales page per day converting at an average 1%).

No guaranteed results of course.

And here's the kicker – even if you can't sell it for $197, you could now 'effortlessly' sell it for $47.

Disclaimer: Don't ever apply this tactic if you know that your product does not have quality content. You're just increasing the value for how much you should be paid so that you're not underpaid for your content. :-)

49. A DIFFERENT WAY OF THINKING TO MAKE LOTS OF MONEY ONLINE

People fail to make money online because they think way too much about making money online.

No, I'm not asking you not to think about yourself - I'm just asking you to also **think about your prospect's interest**. Why would they want to buy from you?

If you know that answer, you're already half way to making money for yourself.

The answer should be because you're selling VALUE instead of some stupid promise that you've been sold in the past by those snake oil marketers.

You see, **when you start thinking about your prospects, your product offer will naturally become better**, which of course, will give you better sales conversion.

The next part that I want to touch on is building businesses.

If a Newbie can just understand that he is building a business, he will be successful. Unfortunately, he thinks the Internet is a cash machine (see what these garbage marketers have done with their promises to honest people?) and that he just needs to unlock some weird code for the Internet to spit money out at him.

Crazy, I know. But guess what - many bought into this promise.

Click a button = unlimited traffic. And you just need to spend 30 bucks for that piece of software. Cool isn't it?

You know what, such software does exist but it's definitely not 30 bucks and you still have to do some work.

Put on your thinking cap - if it's only 30 bucks, the guy who's selling the software would probably sell you the traffic (the golden egg) rather than sell you the software (the golden goose) for the price of dinner for two at California Kitchen Pizza.

So that's why people think that the Internet doesn't 'work.' "After a week of testing, nothing happened so I'll throw in the towel. It's all BS." All this garbage on the internet kills honest people's dreams. Sad.

But if the Newbie knows that he's building a business and is **excited about that**, he won't give up.

I'll tell you why he should be excited...

Never before, in any part of the world, have ordinary people, been able to start a real business SO FAST at such a low cost of entry.

I just set up another new internet business, an online store, and it was completed in less than a week and ranked in the search engine for the main keyword on day 7. It has nothing to do with the internet marketing niche. (Perhaps I'll share my model in my new course next year.)

Imagine if I was to do this offline, the conventional business way I'll have to register for a company, find a store to rent, go through business documentations, renovate the store to fit my product, buy inventories, hire employees (at least 3), manage people, prepare promotions and so on.

If I could get everything up in 45 days, I would be thankful. And that's not even including the marketing, getting people to my store. But the worst part is, I'll probably spend a bare minimum of $10K to get things setup. Plus, it's demographic restricted, so my income ceiling is capped.

So remind me again, why wouldn't I be extremely excited about building a real online business?

In all, the Internet is working very well. Just understand what I've shared with you and you'll begin to focus on the right thing to make money online.

50. HOW TO HAVE 78% OPT-IN CONVERSION

If you're long in the internet marketing niche, you'll know that conversion at 78% is VERY HIGH. Anyone getting 40% will probably be celebrating. I know this to be true because most of the launches that I've promoted normally convert at less than 34% on their squeeze pages or opt-in pages.

A little bit of history for the case study – this is an opt-in page for a new product I've launched at www.youchanbewealthy.com which has NOTHING to do with internet marketing. Other than selling in the internet marketing niche, I have several other online businesses – especially those in niche markets that are not exposed.

"Do you want to know how to increase your opt-in conversion based on real life proof?"

The common tip you'll hear is on the site design and the copy. I would say that's true, in general. But it's not the universal truth because if you were to 'steal' someone's converting page and copy for your own use, there's no guarantee you'll get the same conversion. This is simply because you do not know the mechanism going on at the back. Does that make sense? It'll help, but I wouldn't bet on its success.

It's what your copy's promising – **THE OFFER.** What will they get if they decide to subscribe?. I've also conducted a test of numerous offers – giving more free gifts to get visitors to subscribe DOES NOT equal to higher conversion. And even if they do, what are the chances that they'll remain as your subscriber or read your future messages?

The main concern you need to focus on for getting higher opt-in conversion is identifying the traffic source.

Just realizing this will make you richer. Put it this way – if your opt-in page is about 'golf swings' and it is being read by a golf player, he'll be more likely to subscribe than a car mechanic. Focus only on targeted traffic sources. They'll be more likely to subscribe and buy from you at later stage. This is 'basic' but most people ignore it because it's more 'exciting' to get traffic.

The next part is, your **credibility**. You can use stupid copy and you'll still get people to subscribe if you're known for giving real value.

Credibility has a lot to do with relationships – how you connect with your website visitors and previous subscribers. If they've gained great content from your site or list, they'll be more likely to subscribe, regardless of whether you'll be promoting any products to them.

Just to make everyone aware of why bumping up conversion is so critical, assume you get 1,000 visitors. If your conversion is only 20%, you'll be getting 200 new subscribers.

If you can increase it to 50%, that's an extra 300 subscribers into your list. Assuming you stick to only 20% conversion, it'll take you 2,500 visitors to get the same result as a 50% conversion page.

And let's say, it'll just cost you $0.20 cent per click from Facebook ads - that's an extra $300 cost which you can use to pay for your hosting, autoresponder, shopping cart, etc. EACH MONTH.

Now, just increase 1,000 to 10,000 over a period of time - you'll end up spending $3,000.

But if you work on your conversion each time you want to build a mailing list, it'll take less effort to make it right in the first place.

51. SOCIAL MEDIA LIES

There are two groups of people who will not like reading what I have to write in this chapter today - first, those who are looking for the magic pill to get massive Facebook fans. Secondly, those social media "experts" who are pushing their courses and solutions for the magic pill (I guess this second group will not only dislike what I'll be saying, but angered).

Before I start my rant, I have a quick question... do you realize that *almost* everyone is claiming to be a social media/Facebook expert nowadays?

Because they feel like they know how to use (or play) Facebook, they're labeling themselves as the "experts.". Even many "experts" or social media companies are NOT experts, despite if they do it for Nestle or Angelina Jolie (you'll understand why after reading this chapter).

It's rather simple to brand themselves as "Facebook experts" or "digital media companies" because these terms are vague -- if you call yourself a best-selling author, you need to BE a best-selling author. If you call yourself an internet millionaire, you need to BE an internet millionaire. If they call themselves as "Facebook experts" it's hard to argue because it requires no substance to claim it.

Here's the harsh reality -- there is no magic pill that will allow you to have hundreds of thousands of fans on your Facebook fan page, period. Read all of the courses you want, attend all of the seminars you need... you won't find that magic pill.

So how do they get massive fans, then?

The thing is, unless you are a celebrity or a well-known brand, you will not be able to accumulate the number of fans that these fan pages have. If you are an ordinary person (meaning, without the Angelina Jolie brand), you'll spend money to get fans, particularly through buying Facebook ads, and you'll end up a broke marketer if you don't have a strategy in place to monetize on them. Then we have problem #2 - how to monetize?

Let's talk about "celebrities.". I was with a famous model celebrity recently and when I checked out her Fan Page, she has over 200,000 fans! Now, I could be wrong, but I doubt she runs Facebook ads or does any aggressive fan page marketing. Amber Chia has a lot of fans because she IS Amber Chia. You got that? There is no magic pill.

There are Facebook marketers who sell their courses by displaying how they helped celebrities or big brands. But come on... do you think it's their strategies or because Starbucks AUTOMATICALLY attract fans on its own? You be the judge.

Just to give credits to these experts, even if the success is because of the strategies, there are almost no unique strategies there - **post awesome content, invite engagement and get them to share with others.** You and I cracked that code a long time ago.

Sure, there are so many so-called "social media" experts who teach you how to make big bucks with social media.

But what you should be asking these experts is whether they have a lot of fans on their fan pages. If you check their fan pages, you'll notice that they don't have so many fans after all.

And if they do, is there any engagement or are there just Likes bought at Fiverr?

It's really funny seeing all of these Facebook "gurus" or social media "experts" pitching how awesome their software is and talking AS IF they know Fan Page marketing enough to get 100,000 or 1,000,000 fans. Then they pitch to you, asking you to pitch to local businesses the same s*#t promises! Funny crap.

So there is no real secret to getting a lot of fans on Facebook.

Actually, there's no secret but there are MARKETING STRATEGIES.

There are Fan Pages created by ordinary people that have gotten viral and been liked by 100,000 fans. The fact is, in any niche or industry, there will always be exceptions - Harry Potter, Angry Birds and so on. Thousands of authors tried and failed. Thousands of games developed and failed. Make sense? So all of the Smart Alecs out there who are reading this chapter, please don't be a Smart Alec and say that there are cases of successes out there - I know that.

To wrap up...

A Facebook fan page is a fantastic platform but there is just no magic pill that will allow you to have 100,000 fans in a short time. If you just want to make some money, sure, Fan Page can help you to do that. I'm doing that as well.

So stop thinking "how did Tony Robins or Starbucks get so many fans" -- the answer is because they are Tony Robbins and Starbucks. But here's the kicker... nobody said that you cannot be a "celebrity" or "brand," unless you're not willing to commit to your own business and start putting up a Fan Page to build relationships.

Note: If you want to know how I use social media:

www.socialstrategic.com

52. IF YOU CAN'T WRITE AN EBOOK

If writing an eBook is too much for you, write a small report to sell online.

For an example, let's say you sell weight loss information. Here's an example of the types of reports and eBooks you might create:

- $10 report that gives an overview of nutrition and exercise guidelines.
- $50 eBook that gives more in-depth information on losing weight.
- $100 eBook package that offers advanced weight-loss information.
- $40 eBook about motivation.
- $30 eBook about maintenance.
- $15 report about weight loss supplements.
- $10 report about getting flat abs.

You get the idea. You can offer a variety of products under a variety of price points, so that you always have "something else" to sell to your prospects as well as your existing customers.

Here's the profitable part...

Turn the short report into a monthly membership. One of the main advantages of building a membership site is that it gives you the opportunity to create a passive income stream.

That's because you sell your prospects once on joining your membership site, and then they keep paying recurring monthly membership fees, which generates residual income for you.

Each month, your members get a report. Simple as that.

And here's the idea to automate it:

Drip content membership. This style of site is like a traditional membership site, because you provide a new report to your members and they pay you ongoing membership fees. The difference, however, is that you've made it clear upfront that this arrangement only lasts for a fixed term, such as three months, six months, a year or more.

The advantage is that you won't struggle as much with member retention, because people who start a membership site and see a clear end date in the future are less likely to quit. They'll just stick it out in order to get the full benefits of your training materials.

Another advantage is that you can create the reports once and have them delivered by autoresponder, which makes the day-to-day maintenance largely hands-free for you.

53. HOW TO EXPAND YOUR MARKET

Assuming you've already gotten started in your market, you may want to reach other markets too. And it's easier than you think.

That's because you don't need to start from scratch with your products and marketing materials. All you need to do is "niche-ify" your content.

Niche-ifying refers to taking one product (and the accompanying marketing materials) and tweaking it to appeal to a different niche market.

Example: Let's say you sell a course that teaches other people how to write and sell eBooks. And maybe you're currently targeting internet marketers, so the book is geared towards those who want to create the eBooks and sell them online. In other words, it's a traditional "how to make money" online course.

Now let's look at how a few tweaks to the course, the sales letter, and other marketing materials can allow you to quickly and easily reach other niche markets:

- Stay at home moms. Maybe stay at home moms aren't looking to make a full time income. After all, they already have a full time job (raising their children), but perhaps they're just looking for a way to pick up an extra $500 or $1000 a month. You can tweak your book and sales materials to appeal to this niche.

- Novelists. Here you can take your existing content and tweak it to appeal

128

to writers who're looking to reach their markets digitally. This includes teaching people how to sell their books via Amazon's Kindle marketplace.

- People in specific fields wanting to reach specific markets. Here you can teach information marketers in specific niches how to create an eBook and sell it. For example, you can teach personal trainers how to write and sell fitness eBooks to their clients.

Perhaps at this point you're starting to wonder what I mean by "tweaking" the content to appeal to specific niches. Let me give you an example…

Let's say you're taking your general course and niche-ifying it to appeal to stay at home moms. Here are some changes you might make:

- Change the title from "The Online Marketer's Guide to Writing and Selling an EBook" to "The Stay-At-Home-Mom Guide to Writing and Selling an EBook."

- Change the headline of your sales letter to something like, "Attention All Stay at Home Moms Who Could Use an Extra $500 Every Month…"

- Gear the sales letter towards stay-at-home-moms, by addressing the fact that they only have a few hours here and there to work while the baby is sleeping or the children are quietly playing.

- Tweak the content of the book itself, by creating a new chapter about time management and productivity for busy moms.

- Place your ads where stay-at-home-moms will see them, such as on parenting boards.

Those are just a few examples. The point is that you need to tweak all the content so that your new niche feels like you created the course just for them.

54. LAW OF SCARCITY IN MARKETING

Scarcity can generate higher demand to your product. We all know that.

We tend to think that if something is limited or rare in quantity – then it has to be valuable. People hate to lose any opportunity to change their life and may have to resist not trying your offer. "For limited time only" is a well-known marketing tactic to trigger the scarcity factor.

For instance, if you collect coins, the more rare the coin is, the more valuable it is. The rarest coins can be sold for a lot of money and the demand for it can be huge. The price rises because of the higher demand.

So how do you apply this law into marketing?

Apply this in a product launch.

You'll start by giving people free content and testimonials and all other elements from the sales page. You're giving it in small chunks to make people interested and intrigued about your product. There is a deadline set up, with exact date and time.

At the end of the product launch there is limited time only, limited quantity, limited low price scarcity rule employed.

Product launches are open mostly for just few days and sell hundreds of high-ticket programs in a matter of days. Because a lot of products in product launches are coaching-based, there is easy justification for why it's limited.

In addition to building a bigger event around the product, people employ the pre-launch tactic of the 'special list' broadcast message, 10 minutes before, with a 'secret link' to get cool bonuses or discounts. That's why you are seeing 6 to 7 figures revenue generated in 2 hours launches. It exploits scarcity factor perfectly.

Learn from these launches and employ it in your own marketing. It's indeed one of the most powerful weapons ever discovered in online marketing.

Product launch is the "secret weapon" of creating scarcity.

55. THE SECRET TO INTERNET MARKETING?

So what is the secret to internet marketing? Or to ANY other online business success?

It's actually being stated clearly to us, in front of our face – it's MARKETING. The truth is, it's about having a powerful marketing strategy for your internet business. If you're confused by what I mean, let me explain...

You see, these "Gurus" talk about their blogging software, keyword software, traffic software or Facebook software, or any of those "push button" software that SUPPOSEDLY generate income for you... they'll sell you those shinning objects that promise to make $14,321 in 5 days or something similar.

Truth is, they don't use those "push button" software to make hundreds of thousands or a million. They're using the "REAL STUFF" - which is none other than effective marketing strategy.

Even if "push button" stuff works, they must to be "combined" with a marketing strategy.

Look at all of the great businesses today - they have a particular strategy that makes them so successful today.

On the large scale, let's look at:

Microsoft. Bill Gates understands the strategy of LEVERAGE and "joint venture". He rides on IBM by "incorporating" Windows into computers.

Facebook. Targeting University students when it was first launched. Novelty. "Exclusivity". Niche selection.

Google. Way too many strategies to list here but one that is paramount would probably is focusing on giving good stuff away for free.

If you're doing internet marketing, the #1 strategy you must use is "information marketing".

The reason is that you can use valuable information to powerfully generate leads, as bonuses to your physical or other information products, to build credibility, to sell them separately and so on.

So the biggest question would probably be this... how do I learn marketing strategies?

Of course the simplest strategy is to learn from a mentor. But this opportunity doesn't always exist so here are others for you to consider:

1. Look at how big companies are launching their "products." Try to decode what marketing strategy they're applying, and then see how that can be applied into your own business. I thought of the strategy of giving away products for free simply based on what I've observed from Google. I'm not a genius, I'm just good at observing.

2. Look at how your competitors are doing it. If you're in the information business, the best place to find them is at Clickbank.com. Read their sales letters. Watch their video sales letters. You'll learn how they sell. Go through their product launch.

3. Create your own "mastermind" group. This way, whenever you have thought of a marketing strategy, you can bounce your idea off of them to see if they like it or not.

But here's what I think would be the greatest "marketing strategy" of all time:

"Choose your market wisely; choose the market that will be responsive toward your message and focus on building relationships with them. The goal is not trying to sell your product, but positioning yourself as the person who will help them solve their problems. This way, they will appreciate your . product/service because you're adding value to them."

56. HOW TO TAP INTO MOBILE MARKETING

The fact is, mobile marketing is becoming more evident, and what's interesting is that it's also VERY EFFECTIVE.

The first lesson - think of it as an extended marketing channel for your existing business.

For instance, if you have an online or offline business, you put up a Fan Page. Why? Well... sometimes, people put that up because "everyone" has it. :) But it's mainly because it's an extended marketing channel for you to reach your existing prospects and NEW prospects, even if it doesn't generate revenue on its own.

When it comes to mobile apps, these are the 2 thoughts that come to mind:

i. Sell the app to make money
ii. Display ads in the app to make money

Although both of the above are correct, most marketers are missing out using it as an **extended marketing channel.**

So I thought of writing this article to share a real life case study of how effective mobile marketing can be…

You see, I've been quietly promoting in the self-improvement niche in Google Play Store under the radar. Actually, in Apple Appstore too. If you search for "self-improvement," you'll see my app there. Of course, depending on when you're reading this, the ranking may have changed.

Anyway, back to the marketing strategy…

I'm not trying to make money from the app - it's simply an extended marketing channel for me to "stay in touch" with my existing loyal subscribers and also, a platform to get new leads EVERY DAY (the app gets new downloads every day).

A while ago, I also started playing around with another marketing channel - Amazon Kindle. So when my book was available there, I emailed my subscribers, shared on my Facebook Fan Page and so on to tell them about the book launch.

And at the same time, I use mobile marketing - I simply sent out a "push notification" to more than 10,000 smartphones (including iPhone users). Now, think of it this way –

You're on your iPhone. Suddenly, you get a notification to your phone. It's very unlikely you don't open it, so you open it up to read the message. Here's the message:

FREE AMAZON BOOK: Patric has just released The Simple Success Principles Book and he's giving it for free at Amazon today! Only available free for ONE DAY, get it at {LINK}

This goes without saying, it automatically boost lots of downloads for my book in Amazon within 24 hours.

In fact, it was #1 for Top Free 100 in the best-seller list under the self-help category, "Happiness".

3 key things about mobile app marketing that beat any other marketing medium:

1. **It can happen in real-time.** If you're running a business (online or offline) that needs attention ASAP, nothing can reach people faster than mobile marketing, period.

2. **High frequency of consumption.** If an app is valuable (as in useful, entertaining, etc.), it gets to be used frequently. If you're promoting something that requires several times of exposure, this does the job for you.

3. **It's cheap.** In my case, it's free because I'm getting app downloads from the Appstore. But relatively, advertising in mobile network is cheap (for now).

57. STRATEGIC VS. TACTICAL

I think I wrote about this on my blog some time ago, but it's worth the time to share it in this book.

There's a huge different between being strategic and tactical. Both of them have their own time and places to be used. I think it's easier to explain by giving an example rather than explaining the concept itself...

Assuming a marketer is trying to increase the conversion of his product sales.

Tactical: When the visitor exits, a popup appears to give $10 discount. Does this increase conversion? Likely. I mean, who doesn't like to get discount. So it WORKS. But 2 new problems arise –

i.   The marketer loses the trust. He's rewarding his prospects for LEAVING, instead of for being "supportive" in taking action. Would you like to buy from this kind of merchant? Personally, I would have a second thought. On a separate note, trust is *everything* in business, especially in the "how to" teachings industry.

ii.   It will not work for long term. After a while, prospects will get "smart" at this tactic and you're "training" them to exit your website.

Strategic: A strategic marketer knows the goal - it's to increase the conversion. He can still have a popup, but instead of offering discount, he could offer a real valuable free gift in return for subscribing. Then he will increase the conversion through email follow ups by "educating" the prospects of what the product can do for them (or what they can achieve from the product).

Does this mean thats tactical is wrong and we should always be strategic?

Not really. Because Bbeing tactical does work and it can usually help a marketer to get instant results or make money fast. Tactical is usually associated withto methods of making money online, whereas else, being strategic would usually leads to building a business.

Tactics usually change., Yyou'll need to adapt to new tactics every time. There are many tactics to get ranked in Google.com and you should use them to gain the unfair advantage against your competitor.

On the other hand, strategies are usually evergreen. To get ranked in Google.com, by being strategic would simply mean doing what Google wants you to do for them. For instance, Wikipedia.org doesn't seems to have the need to do SEO optimization;, it's ranked well because they're giving what Google wants -- accurate content for of what people are searching for.

The best method is to always by combinening BOTH OF THEM.

For instance, I'm wrote a book in the self improvementself-improvement niche called, "WakeUp Millionaire". We'll use all kinds of tactics to promote it, like using a powerful sales letter, discount on launch date, adding bonuses, etc.

The strategy would be building the brand, creating a system for it to continue growing for years and so on.

In summary, be strategic but remember to apply powerful tactics in your business.

58. A NEW PLACE TO GET TARGETED TRAFFIC

Sometimes, you need to be creative to find out where your customers are.

Forums are one of the best places to reach them and most marketers do not realize that they can buy advertising there! It's highly targeted because you're not putting your ad in front of casual one-time visitors. Instead, you're putting your ads in front of highly targeted repeat visitors.

What's more, you're putting your ads in front of a community who cares about the forum and its owner.

Many regular, loyal forum visitors will purchase from a forum's "sponsors" just as a way to support the forum. That means that if you pick the right forum (one with a lot of loyal, regular visitors), you'll likely enjoy a responsive audience.

Different forums allow different types of advertising, including text ads and banner ads. These text and banner ads may appear on the main forum page, between forums or even between posts. You may:

- Pay a per-month, flat-fee rate for the ad.
- Pay per click for the ad.
- Pay per impression for the ad.

So how do you find these forums? The easiest way is to run a Google search for your keywords alongside words like "keyword+forum," where you'll replace the keyword with the words that describe your niche market.

Tip: Be sure to only place your ads on targeted, high-quality forums. Some forums are basically advertising forums, where people come to place ads and that's it. Avoid these and stick with popular communities that accept advertising.

However, keep in mind that just because a forum doesn't specifically offer forum advertising opportunities doesn't mean they aren't open to it. This is especially true if you see a forum using something like Google AdSense or affiliate links. This shows that they're open to advertising but perhaps they've just never considered selling the ad space directly.

Getting an ad on these types of sites is as simple as asking. And the bonus is that you won't have a lot of competition with other advertisers (at least in the beginning).

You can send an email to them, with a template like this:

Subject: I'd like to purchase ad space on [forum name]

Dear [forum owner's name],

Hi, my name is [your name] and I am seeking out advertising opportunities for my site [name and link]. I noticed that you have affiliate links and Google AdSense on your forum. Would you consider selling flat-rate ad space for a [banner ad/text ad] directly to me?

The benefit is that you'll make money even if no one clicks on the ad. You don't have to worry about making a few pennies per click or trying to pre-sell someone on an affiliate product. You get easy income just by selling ad space to me.

Please hit reply now or call me at [phone number] to tell me your ad rates. I look forward to working with you!

[Your Name]

Or you can even go to www.buysellads.com to find those forums who are selling banner ads.

Start seeing traffic come to your site! ☺

59. MOST FAIL TO MAKE EVEN A DOLLAR ONLINE

If you look carefully, making money online boils down to mastering 3 core things -- you need to have a website and a valuable product to offer, and you need to get traffic to it.

And yet, in this industry, most fail to even make a dollar online!

It's actually not surprising at all. If you study the situation carefully, you'll soon discover that those who failed are those who jump on the internet with the wrong "understanding" of what they're going to get.

In fact, it's the same direct-selling/MLM stuff. They join because they were introduced by their "uplines" and told how much money they can make by just recruiting 3 downlines. So what happened? You've probably been down that road, so go figure.

People jump on the Internet thinking it's like an ATM cash machine or something. Some even think it's like lottery. Some have the impression that they can make $10,000 or even $50,000 within the next 30 days, from "nothing".

Look – the Internet is not that It's merely a channel to promote a business. However, this channel allows extreme leverage, low cost and "unlimited" reach.

Get excited about the Internet because it CAN transform your financial life, but don't be ignorant.

Nothing's going to happen after you've put up a website. You're not going to get 100,000 visitors if you're not PAYING for your traffic or not spending a lot of time promoting it. In my world, there's no way you can make money if other people are not giving you money *willingly*. Thus, stop thinking about how you're going to make money and start thinking of what VALUE you can give. Then figure out how you can show this value to customers.

60. HOW TO USE AMAZON FOR PRODUCT CREATION IDEAS

Magazines, top selling books and that infamous store – Amazon – are some of the best research tools out there. When people spend money on magazines and books they're spending money on information.

Sometimes it's "hard information" on how to do something.

Sometimes it's softer information, more entertaining or what you might call "infotainment".

A lot of hobby magazines and books fall into this category.

Surf on over to Amazon because there are few retailers better when it comes to displaying the HOT topics that people are paying for – and more importantly – paying for online.

Amazon isn't just a great place to get ideas on information that's selling… it's a great way to start building your product and see what your customers are REALLY thinking.

It's vital you keep in touch with your market. After all, they're the ones spending money, so learn as much as you can about what they're doing, saying and thinking.

You can look for niches and take short-cuts through the book and magazine sections to have a quick glance at headlines and niches. For instance, there is always a range of magazines on Home & Garden.

Here's another trick:

Let's take fitness training as an example...

Fitness people, Cyclists, golfers – they are all the same – they'll spend money on equipment and ways to improve their game.

So strolling over to the Amazon marketplace and going through Best Sellers in the Sports section, I find a book on Barefoot Running (of course, by the time you're reading this book, it'll be a different book at #1).

Here's how we go 'Undercover at Amazon' and let them do the hard work for us...

The product page for books usually has a nice big **"Click to LOOK INSIDE!"** option at the top right side of the book cover.

Inside you'll get to look at the table of contents and even read some of the pages. This is perfect "Inside Information" on the authors thoughts on what's important and what people want to read.

The Barefoot Running book has a particularly nice layout with sections and chapters. This is where you need to start thinking about specific problems.

You don't need to create a whole book - you can always find a section (ideally the hottest section) and focus your product on that and nothing else.

Lastly...

You can read customer reviews at Amazon.

They'll tell you exactly what they liked, what they didn't like, if the product was any good, and even recommend alternatives.

You can really connect with the market here. Look at the words they use, the jargon, the slang and so on. If you learn to speak their language then selling your product will be 10 times easier.

So the next time you head over to Amazon.com, consider using it as a marketing research tool too.

61. HOW TO BLOG WITHOUT WRITING

Let's say that you create an amazing blog on a certain niche. It is getting tons of traffic and making you a lot of money. By that time you have spent a ton of time creating the content and getting readers!

What do you do when you want to stop writing on that topic and move onto something else?

That is when you get stuck because you are the PRODUCT.

You can't really sell the site for what it's worth because you will no longer be creating the content. The people who visit your blog regularly come to hear what you have to say. Take you out of the equation and the value of what you built is gone.

The key to building a profitable blog is that it becomes a business/asset.

It should be able to be sold at any second for top dollar because you aren't the sole content provider. I am not saying that you can't write for the blog, but you can't be the main content provider.

TechCrunch.com was sold for $30,000,000. That is roughly 36X the monthly revenue that they were doing. The guy who started the site was the original author on the blog. Before he sold the site he was very rarely posting on the site. He recruited other people who were passionate about technology to write for his site and that turned TechCrunch into an asset that could be sold for big bucks.

The idea is to create a blog which allows "guest bloggers.".

You can consider using www.blogsynergy.com to simply find independent writers from their own blogs.

The idea here is to use other people's writing for your blog – instead of you being the blogger. Something worth pondering.

To find out more about blogging business, go to **www.blogging.guru**

62. 5 BLOGGING SECRETS TO GET READERS

I'm going to share with you how you can get blog readers to read your blog more often.

I'm not going to talk about getting more traffic in this training because that is self explanatory. It's like telling you if you need to lose weight you have to eat less and exercise more. Obviously for you to get readers to your blog, you have to drive traffic there.

But once you have visitors, or to be more precise readers, how do you get them to read your blog more often?

Here are the 5 secrets...

1.   Listen To Your Readers

This does not mean that you listen to them literally. You can't do that because they can't convey any messages to you via audio.

In this case it means listen to what they are saying or what they are telling you.

This can be done by simply reading the comments that they leave for you.

The first option I gave you is to get them to leave their comments. Here, some of them actually leave their comments voluntarily. Read those comments and you'll probably be able to pick up some valuable tips.

Some of the comments may be saying that your blog contains really good stuff and how much they love certain posts. Those are all signs that they like what they are reading.

Then there are people who don't leave any comments. If you're not getting comments when you should, then maybe you'll want to consider that the blog post that you put up is not getting any readership. This tells you that you've got the wrong stuff on your blog.

This cannot be a universal rule because sometimes people just don't leave comments. I'm just saying that you can gauge your readers' response simply by reading the comments that they leave on your blog.

2.   Go To Forums

This is a great way for you to generate blog entry ideas.

When you're there you can search for your topic and see the trends from forums. From there you're going to get so many cool ideas on what people are talking about. Most likely, whatever they are talking about in the forums is stuff that you can blog about. You will be able to generate all kinds of ideas.

Let's say a person in the forum is posting about his problem with his girlfriend. Maybe his girlfriend has another boyfriend or something like that. If you happen to be in the dating niche, you've just got an idea for a blog post about how to get your girlfriend back if she falls in love with another guy.

By going to forums, you're going to get a lot of ideas.

3.   Newspapers & Magazines

This is something that you might not think about because we are so engaged with this internet world that everything has to be done online. We do our research, etc online.

We forget the source of content that we have in our hands every single day - newspapers and magazines.

Flip through your magazines and newspapers and, I kid you not, you're going to get some ideas from there.

Let's take dog training as an example. You don't know what to write about on your blog regarding dog training. Go to your bookstore and check out a dog training magazine. I'm sure there are dog or pets magazines out there.

I'm sure you can't argue with me that you can't find good content or ideas from a magazine.

4.   Respond To Your Comments

Your readers put all these comments on your blog. They tell you what they like and don't like, and some bloggers don't reply. That's just crazy. When people leave comments, they are starting a conversation with you. You have to start leaving your responses to their comments so that there is a real conversation going on. That's how marketing works.

Today, marketing is no longer a one way channel. It's a conversation that you must adapt to.

So you're going to use your blog as an opportunity to have a conversation with your readers.

Respond to as many comments as you can. Of course this does not mean that you respond to every single comment. Here's what I'll do. If I have 5 comments, I'll reply with a single comment that addresses all 5 of them.

5.   Be Controversial

You can occasionally post something controversial but that is not ethically shooting anyone down.

For example, let's say your blog is about internet marketing.

In one of your posts, you might say that Twitter is a waste of time and that whoever is using it is wasting their time.

On a side note, that's going to irritate a lot of people because a lot of people think that Twitter is the next big thing for them to make money on the internet.

When you do a controversial post, people automatically respond to it. It's just human behavior. There is nothing magical about it. It's just that people have to respond to it.

Controversial basically means contradicting what is actually happening, not to a particular person. The last thing you want to do is create enemies or accidentally shoot someone down.

Don't say that a particular product is not good or that something a particular person said, teaches, or blogs about is bad.

All you have to do is say something very generic. At the same time, when you write something controversial, you must have some solid proof to back up what you say. You always want to use words like, "I feel", "I think" or "In my personal opinion." Don't make an across the board type of statement. I just want you to be careful about that. This is a very powerful tactic but I really don't want you to use it the wrong way.

Check out **www.blogging.guru**

63. LEVERAGED INTERNET MARKETING

Creating your own product gives you amazing leverage.

This fundamental comes from both personal experience and reason. Here's why you need to create your own products...

Your Sales Funnel From Front End To Back End

In Leveraged Internet Marketing, your first step is to start getting prospects into your sales funnel at a rapid pace.

Your sales funnel is simply a system you use to capture leads and sell to them over and over again.

It's said that for every lead you get into your sales funnel, you make $1 a month. So if you have a list of 500, you should be making $500 a month. I actually find that I can make more than this because my list is generated from targeted places and I'm always in personal contact with them (I care about their concerns).

So what's the first step in your sales funnel and how can you use Leveraged Internet Marketing to snag a large amount of customers quickly?

The first step is using a bait piece to get opt-ins to your list. Write a report, create an mp3, or create a video or software, and give it away in exchange for an opt-in.

From opt-in, you send your prospect through your sales funnel. It doesn't have to be anything exact. But here's an example of up selling back end products throughout your sales funnel.

Exchange Bait Piece For Opt-in >

Pitch $7 Report >

Pitch $17 eBook >

Pitch $27 Info Product >

Pitch $47 Info Product >

Pitch $97 Info Product >

Pitch Affiliate Products >

Coaching and Consulting >

I will offer upsell, but I'll also offer downsell of my back end products. The point is, selling through your sales funnel on the back end from week-to-week helps you sustain your income. Don't depend on your front end products. You'll make money off of them, but leverage them to form joint ventures so you can get more customers into your sales funnel. Got it?

Here are a few ways to generate leads (opt-ins) quickly:

1. Create a report and sell it for $7. For instance, this report can be sold for $7. You offer 100% commissions to affiliates for your $7 report and each time you sell, you add a buyer to your sales funnel.

2. Write a report with your best stuff and give it away through a paid advertisement. Make prospects opt-in to get the report, so you can send them through your sales funnel. A lot of people give away reports without having them opt-in for it. While this could be effective in the long run, it's not Leveraged Internet Marketing. If you run a $20 ad and get over 100 opt-ins, that money was well spent.

3. Make custom squeeze pages as the bridge between almost everything you sell. Before the prospect can get to your sales page, put a squeeze page there (as and when it's possible).

Position Your Product By Building & Setting Value

Positioning your product has to do with the perceived value you build in your prospect's mind.

Positioning in selling information products is everything, isn't it? Think about it. How is it that a marketer can take roughly the same information that's in a $29.95 book you can get at Barnes & Nobel and sell it for $497 as a course?

I know what you're thinking. You might think this extreme case is unethical. But it's not and here's why.

Selling information is much different than selling physical products. For example, Colgate toothpaste will always have the same perceived value. You can't take a bottle of Colgate toothpaste and sell it for $100. No one would buy.

With information, it's much different. You can set and build a perceived value for the information in your prospect's mind. Because you're not really selling an eBook, mp3s, or videos - you're selling information, and information normally has more value than what's even put on it!

Information can be worth more than $1,000,000. One paragraph in an eBook can make somebody $1,000,000, but I doubt he paid that much money for the eBook. So the information in that eBook all together is worth well-over $1,000,000. You follow?

If someone wrote the secret to life on a napkin, how much would that be worth to you? It's not about the physical napkin (or eBook, audio, video). It's about the value of the information.

YOU set the value of the information you're selling in your prospect's mind. This is positioning your product. And you want to position it at a high perceived value even if you're selling it for much less.

Start Leveraged Internet Marketing.

64. 4 WAYS TO GET YOUR OPT IN SUBSCRIBERS TO TRUST YOU QUICKLY

While the rest of the world have developed many barriers and protections to keep their e-mail accounts spam-free, there are also those that subscribe to mailers that promote their products, services and their site.

This is mainly because these subscribers want to know more about what these sites are offering and can be beneficial for them. They expect to get be kept posted on what they are interested in and what is new in the market or field they have chosen.

You would be so lucky to have these kinds of customers; the basic element needed to get these types of people is trust.

When your customers trust you they will reward you with their loyalty.

To build a good opt-in list you need people to trust you, for a faster and quicker build up, you need to get your opt-in subscribers to trust you quickly. The faster you build your opt-in list the faster word about you and your site gets to be spread. The bigger the scope of your opt-in list the more traffic you get, spelling more profits.

Its easy math if you think about it. Getting the numbers is not that simple though, or maybe it is?

- Getting the trust of your subscribers shouldn't be so hard especially if you do have a legitimate business. Getting your customers' trust should be based upon your expertise. People rely on other people who know what they are talking about. Frankly if you decide to go into a business, most probably you have an interest in it.

- Show your subscribers that you know what you are talking about. Provide them with helpful hints and guidelines that pertain to what you are selling. You don't have to be a big corporation to make use of an opt-in list. If your customers see you as someone who knows what he is doing and saying, they will trust you quickly.

  •

- Be true to your customers, if you want to hype up your products and services, provide guarantees. The more satisfied customers you get, the bigger probability there is that they will recommend you. Generally, people will trust someone they know. They will go to your site and check it for themselves and be given a chance to experience what the others have experienced from you, so make sure to be consistent in the service you provide.

  •

- Another tip in getting a customer to trust you quickly is to provide them an escape hatch. Show them that you are not there to trap them. Keep a clean list that would enable them to unsubscribe anytime they want. Elaborate your web form by providing information on how to unsubscribe from the list. Guarantee them that they can let go of the service whenever they want to. Many are wary that they may be stuck for life and would have to abandon their email accounts when they get pestered with spam.

Remember that when you get the trust of your subscribers, don't lose that trust. Because if you do anything with their email addresses like sell them or give them out, you will lose many members of your list.

Extra Tip: The true quickest way to gain the trust of your subscribers is when you are recommended by someone they trust.

65. CAN'T DECIDE A TOPIC? TRY THESE...

Writing an eBook to sell is slightly different:

1. It gives a solution to the reader.
2.
3. It should not take too much of your time.
4.
5. It needs to be easy to read (it's an eBook, not a fiction novel ☺).

But many of my readers can't decide on what topic to start with... so here are some ideas you can play around with...

1. **Making Money.** This one ain't ever gonna go away. We all want to make money (if for no other reason than to be charitable and give it away to someone else) and some of us are half-crazed for information on how to make money.

If you can show people how to make money (in a legal, moral way, of course) I can assure you, they will buy it. I guarantee it.

Internet marketing / doing business online eBooks are some of the hottest information products available anywhere in the world. And for good reason. People want to make more money.

So, show them how to do it.

2. **Self Help / Personal Growth.** Another classic topic for writing is what has commonly been referred to as "self help" or "personal growth." People want to improve their lives. Some struggle with

155

addiction and need help in overcoming the struggle. Other people have low self-esteem or feel depressed. Some people don't know how to deal with relationship problems and want to know how to save their marriage. The list could go on and on.

I'll make you another guarantee: show people how to better their lives and they'll buy from you. No question about it.

We all have things about our personalities that we would like changed. Whether we're shy in public or have a horrible temper or don't know when to keep our mouths shut, there are things we'd like to improve.

In fact, I started my online business from this niche.

3. **Weight Loss / Fitness.** Even though obesity and illness are at the highest levels ever, people are working hard to reclaim their health and fit bodies. Gyms are overflowing with sweaty people and stores are selling out of vitamins left and right. Health and fitness is a writing subject that you can never go wrong with.

The point is this: we, as a society, want to be healthier and we struggle with being out of shape.

It's no wonder that diet and exercise is a multi-billion dollar industry.

Might as well get your piece of the pie.

Of course, HEALTH is a big topic.

4. **Dating / Relationships.** What another great topic for an eBook. There are dozens of ideas you could use for this one that could each become best-sellers...

How to avoid divorce court.
How to make your marriage last forever.
How to be more romantic.
How to pick the perfect mate.
How to get people to notice you.
How to use online matchmaking services.
How to be a great father / mother.
How to be a great husband / wife.
How to raise great kids.

I mean, we could go on and on and on here. There are dozens of ideas for this topic and the information sells like crazy. Why? Because if we have positive, enriching, growing relationships, we are HAPPIER.

5.   Everyday Problems.

Let's face it, we all face problems every day of our lives. And often we don't know where to turn or what to do next.

For example: If someone is facing a taxation problem, do you think they would be interested in finding information on how to avoid it? Of course.

I know of one guy who wrote an eBook about BAD BREATH and is selling the thing like crazy. It's an eBook on BAD BREATH for goodness sake. And yet for folks who are struggling with the problem (and I am told it is a common problem -- I guess I've just been lucky :o) they gladly shell out the $20.00 to find a cure.

Everyday problems. They are a headache for US, but they are a product waiting to be created by YOU.

Think about things that people deal with every day that are annoying and cost money and time.

6.   Hobbies and Crafts.

Hot selling items in any bookstore or online as eBooks, are information products about hobbies or crafts. People love making things themselves and getting the self-gratification of a job well done. You could do some quick research on the Internet to see what some of the most common hobbies and crafts are and come up with some unique ideas.

Some might include woodworking, door wreaths, stained glass and any type of do-it- yourself information. Things like improving your golf game, a guide to stamp collecting, antiques and so forth.

Recreation is a huge part of our lives. We all like to spend time enjoying a hobby, and we spend a lot of money supporting those hobbies as a society.

Hobby related information products are almost always a big hit and certainly warrant consideration when choosing a topic to write about.

66. BE YOURSELF EVEN IF SOME PEOPLE DON'T LIKE IT

It requires you to expect and accept the fact that some people are going to flat out reject you online. If you can't deal with rejection, learn to deal with it.

Trust is a result of people seeing you as a real person willing to share of yourself and not just an automated cloned robot pushing out recycled articles and ads just like everyone else seems to do online.

Part of that has to do with the way you write to your readers. You have to write in a way that it looks personal. Like an actual person sat down and took the time to communicate with them. Every single one of your readers knows you have many hundreds or thousands of subscribers but that doesn't mean that you can't **write like only one person is reading.** In fact, that's what you have to do.

One of the easiest ways I've found to learn how to do this is to look at your database of subscribers and pick one to write your letter to. Just one. Then compose your emails in your email client that's addressed to just that one subscriber.

No matter how many people you write to, only one person is reading your email at a time so it's important that it "sounds" like you're writing to that one person.

Personal stories help as well because they help solidify that fact that you are a real person. There's too much use of the word "we" online. If you're the only person running your business then who is "we"? Carefully remove the stick and relax.

If it's just you, say I or me when you write.

There's nothing wrong with that because again, anything that allows people to picture you having a one on one conversation with them goes a long way towards helping you build a relationship with them.

Now here's the thing…

The more personal you can get your newsletter to look, the more your readers will start to respond to you. You see, you've been told to build your list and send out a newsletter and of course you should, but why should you? Do you know why? Has anyone ever told you why?

The #1 goal is to build a relationship with like-minded people who seek guidance on the way to their goals. Your job is to help them get to wherever they want to go. All people care about is where they want to go and if you can help them get there.

Your job is not to send out a bunch of recycled articles and ads. People don't want that and the thing is, many of them won't unsubscribe when you send them junk. They will just stop listening to you.

So, even though you may appear to have thousands of subscribers, you actually don't because many of them have quit reading. You have to ask yourself, why should anyone care about you or what you have to say or even relate to you and your business?

Do you give them a reason to? If you don't, start.

People don't care about or relate to robots.

They care about and relate to other real people.

Standing out online is a good thing. You need to rise above the crowd and show people why they should be dealing with you over someone else.

If you don't, your competitors will be on equal ground with you and you don't want that. You want a person to see you as having no competition because they feel like they know you and that you are someone who wants to help them achieve their goals.

67. IT'S NOT ALL FUN AND GAMES

There's a common theme among those who begin searching for a way to launch their own work at home business – personal freedom. And I've experienced this, so have many of my successful students today.

Or, it could be that you have a job that pays an amazing salary, but just doesn't fulfill you as much as being your own boss would. There's something missing from life when you're forced to report to a job at a specific time, told what tasks need to be done, and obligated to steer a company the way other people say it should be directed.

Being your own boss doesn't just entail sleeping late and working in your pajamas, as many hyped up products like to lure you with. In fact, you may even find there's more work involved – depending on what path you choose to acquire your wealth.

Now you know about the benefits, let's talk reality about this world of online operations, because there seems to be some great myth that most marketers are promoting pie in the sky dreams that are mostly hype and very little substance.

I know – many authors just sugar coat stuff because they're just trying to sell you their latest widget. To be honest with you, it really doesn't matter if you buy any stuff from me or not, but more importantly, I can help you with the truth.

The reality is – it is work!

You're not going to choose a username, create a link and wake up to $1,000 that you made while you sleep. Even affiliate marketing – where you sell other people's goods, requires you to do some work to get your share of the commission.

If you're looking for a turnkey, get rich quick miracle, infopreneuring or internet marketing isn't it. Go buy a lottery ticket and pray that your numbers win big. You can't see those stats where one guy makes $1 million in 18 hours and think that's going to happen to you in your first week.

Being successful at anything you choose to do requires hard work and consistency. I know that in the Internet marketing field, use of those words is a big no-no, but it's the undeniable truth.

Without an understanding that you may have to work for your success you might think there's some secret formula out there that's going to magically put money in your pockets simply because you know it.

The reality is, it took more than those 18 hours to make that million – it took months, if not a year to get that product launch set up to rake in that much cash in a short period of time.

If you're not going to enjoy the drudgery of getting all your ducks in a row before the money starts rolling in, then this business may not be the business for you.

But if you have the motivation and mindset to become your own boss, taking on the responsibilities that entails, along with reaping the rewards, then you might be a perfect fit to don a new career hat as an Internet marketer.

If your needs are more pressing, then it's advisable that you go out and get a job that has a steady paycheck attached to it. Then, work on building your online business in your spare time until it reaches a level of success where you can afford to turn in your resignation and work toward increasing your earnings over time.

Internet marketing isn't a magic bullet. It can provide you with the financial security, the lifestyle, and the prestige you want out of your career.

So after reading this, are you still in?

If yes, you need to have a swift mindset to be prepared for work. Then success will come to you.

68. HITCHING A RIDE TO SUCCESS

Back in 1848 the "California Gold Rush" began. People came from all over the world to claim their share of the wealth. Now you would think that the people who found the most gold were the wealthiest of the time but that isn't exactly true.

The actual fact of the matter is that the people who consistently became rich were the ones who sold tools to those who were mining for gold. People who never found one ounce of gold bought shovels, rugged jeans and other supplies.

Merchants who sold those tools consistently made money no matter how much gold was found.

Selling the tools people need to do something they want to do will always fill your pockets with cash. This concept always works and it never gets stale like specific marketing strategies.

Try and wrap your mind around the concept and you'll be able to come up with your own techniques to use it with.

When you control the tools people need to do whatever is they want to do, you control the actions they take and that includes how they spend their money. If someone has to go through you to get to their destination faster, you can't help but make money.

You see examples of people selling tools all the time. You just have to pay attention. Notice how many things you can't do unless you pay someone for his or her tool to help you do it.

I Haven't Even Scratched The Surface.

There are so many ways to use the concepts I teach that it literally boggles the mind.

Spend some time thinking about how you can "hitch a ride" with people who are looking to spend money to get to their destination and I'm sure you can come up with more than a few ideas.

When you see people doing something they want to do, think about ways to get them to pay you to help them do more of it.

By doing that, you won't need tons of specific ideas from me because you will be able to come up with your own. I just wanted you to understand the basic idea of how this works.

If you look at it, all the gurus do is "hitch a ride" on your desire for a better life by giving you what you think you need; the latest "secret" marketing ideas, tips and strategies to give you an edge over the competition. If you think you need something else, they'll sell you whatever it is that you've shown an interest in.

In other words, your major competitors (the people you learn from) are constantly trying to figure out what you want to do so they can sell you ideas, techniques and tools to help you do more of it knowing you will always pay for anything you think will get you closer to achieving whatever goals you've set for yourself.

When you buy from one person over another, the only reason you do so is because that person has done a better job (presentation wise) of showing you that what they have to offer will help get you to your goals faster than the other guy.

This idea works when selling any type of product or service. Find out what people want to do (many times this is as easy as asking them) then show them how your product helps them do that.

Always remember that the basis for creating products is to help people do more of something they already want to do. For example, if people want to make more money, instead of simply showing them how, give them an easy way to do it with a minimum amount of effort.

Create something else and keep moving forward.

69. HOW TO CREATE EXPERT CONTENT WITHOUT BEING AN EXPERT

I'm sure by now you're wondering if you aren't the one creating the expert content, where does it come from.

Basically, you're going to find niche experts and set up interviews with them. Those experts will supply the content for you. All you have to do is ask them simple questions then shut up and let them speak.

This is how you get FREE niche audio content.

You may wonder why a niche expert would be willing to share their expertise with you (especially for free), but what you have to understand is that every expert is in the self-promotion business.

They all need exposure for their business which makes them eager to share their expertise through interviews.

You can help them get more exposure. That alone is enough (in many cases) to persuade an expert to agree to an interview. I mean more exposure for them usually translates into more money for them.

You see, this process isn't about you at all. The expert wants exposure so your primary job is to show them how providing you with content will help them get more of it. That's something they're probably already trying to do on their own. You're offering them your help to do something they're already trying to do.

Most find that hard to resist.

The expert gets to present themselves as an expert on their topic to more people (when you market the interview) and you get a free niche product.

Help them promote their information and they should be willing to help you with a quality product you can put out there. The people on that site want to be contacted for interviews because they have products and services they'd like to promote themselves.

You should always approach people with a what you'd like to do for them attitude as opposed to a "Gimme an interview so I can profit from it" angle. Respect the people you want something from.

Just about anyone who has a product to sell wants more exposure for their products and services.

70. THE SECRET TO GETTING PEOPLE TO GIVE YOU MONEY

The people who have been able to succeed and continue to succeed, even when markets change and regulations put most out of business, are the people who have the ability to provide great value.

It's all about delivering VALUE to others to make money online.

Customers exchange their money for value, period.

People, your customers, will give you money in exchange for you giving them value. Do not ever forget this.

They seek value and your job is to provide it to them.

If you can acquire one skill, it should be the skill of providing value to people. The other skill would be "sales".

For now, understand that you must get good at providing value. People buy products they WANT, not what they need. Sure, they might think they need something, but likely they merely want it.

You do not need to sell products people need. Most products or services people need are commodities and are regulated. People need food and water. They need shelter and medical. People do not want to spend a lot on needs. In fact, many believe those needs should be provided free by governments!

What most people spend their money on are "wants".

Anyone can live in a $400 per month apartment, but people buy $500,000 houses.

Do they need that nicer house?

Do they need leather seats in their two cars?

Do they need 15 pairs of shoes or 85 different shirts to wear?

Do they need a wireless keyboard for their computer or iPad?

Online, do people need an information product on how to persuade people... how to lose weight... how to get more dates... how to drive traffic... how to earn six figures... how to grow beautiful roses... or how to improve their golf game?

These are "want" products, not "need" products, and these are the types of products most people spend most of their money on. They see these "wants" as needs sometimes, but they are not needs.

Therefore, to understand value is to understand that people have perceptions of value.

If you can acquire the ability to create great value, then you can earn a fortune in direct response marketing, period. And, value is perception.

71. HOW TO MAKE MONEY ONLINE EVEN WITHOUT HAVING YOUR OWN PRODUCT

There are many ways you can still make money online, even if you do not have a product of your own to sell.

I want you to understand this – so long you have a website that can attract the right visitors, you're on your way to making your first dollar online.

I like to share with you many methods of making money online from just ONE NICHE MARKET. If you've found a niche market, you can "expand" and create multiple streams of internet income! For this book's chapter, we'll use the "education" niche.

AdSense Profits – How To Cash In On It

Education niche = Money.

If you are into AdSense, you probably already know about some of the vast opportunities available within this niche. Good search volume; sky high CPC and all that beautiful stuff that makes the AdSense publisher's heart beat a little faster.

The beauty of this niche for AdSense is that it is full of information seekers, and that is exactly the kind of folks you want for AdSense clicks. Yes, these same people who might visit your Amazon site and make you crazy by purchasing nada are just the kind of people you want on an AdSense site.

These folks are seeking, looking and clicking on all kinds of information related to education, and that can put money into your pocket if you know how to capitalize on it.

The great thing about this niche is that there are so many little subniches that come under the big umbrella of education. You could build tons of profitable sites just in one of these subniches alone! But I want to take it a step further and show you just how broad this niche really is, and how education is a niche that is not just limited to monetizing with AdSense either.

Let's get into the mindset of someone who is an ideal prospect for clicking on AdSense ads. The most important thing to know about them is that they are not seeking to buy, for the most part, but they are looking for more information about a topic.

This could be a mom looking for information about home schooling her children, or for more information on the pros and cons of sending her kids to private vs. public school. Or even for information about helping her child create a science fair project.

It could also be someone who is recently unemployed and looking to get into a stable and well-paid position. Here, they will be seeking out training opportunities that will give them the biggest bang for the buck in the shortest amount of time.

The second part is…

Branching out from your original niche.

For instance, "Scholarships" is another part of education niche.

Every student wants to earn a scholarship to help defray the outrageous cost of a college education. You can help these people by providing the information they are seeking about winning one.

There is absolutely no doubt in my mind that you could center an entire site on the topic of "Scholarships".

Amazon Commission

Don't forget that Amazon probably carries a very nice selection of books related to education.

But of course, you know that books don't make much commission for you, HOWEVER, Amazon is helping you out on the upsell upon checkout. You see, if they buy ANYTHING else on Amazon when they're purchasing the book, you'll earn the commission as well.

Online Education Classes

This is a education sub-niche.

Just look at the number of searches and the number of ads showing!
Nearly any traditional degree program that you can think of can now be completed online. Or, if not the entire degree, good portions of many degrees can be completed online now. All indications are that this trend will increase in the coming years.

Even degrees that you would never think of being offered online are now available.

With the economy being the way it is, more people are opting to stay employed while attending classes. Online classes allow them to complete their classes on their own schedule without having to leave their present jobs. They also save money by not having to commute to classes.

Online classes are here to stay, and you can capitalize on the trend.

Don't forget, online classes are not just for college students; they can also be for high school students. This is a demographic that should not be ignored when you are thinking of building a site centered on online classes.

As with the other education sub-niches, location, location, location is everything. Get those states and cities into your keywords.

You can get these affiliate programs from www.cj.com, www.linkshare.com and other networks out there.

Info-Products From Clickbank.com

Clickbank probably does not come to your mind when thinking about how to monetize the education niche but there are some instantly downloadable study and speed reading guides that might really fit the bill for a student who has finals looming.

At 2am, the options to find study guides in a hurry are limited. This is where you can help with providing a desperate student an option to get his or her hands on the guide they need right away.

Get Paid For leads With CPA Programs

As an alternative to AdSense, you can make some nice money with CPA offers from the same crowd! It never pays to put all of your eggs in one basket, particularly when the basket is called AdSense.

There are a few lower-paying offers found on Commission Junction, and it convinced me it could be a great addition to an AdSense site if done correctly.

The real problem here is that many CPA networks won't let newcomers promote in the education niche right off the bat. It may take you a month or two of working with one of the CPA network's affiliate managers to get to be able to promote these lucrative offers.

If you think you might be interested in eventually adding education CPA offers to your site, it would pay to get your feet wet promoting offers in other niches. This way you will gain the trust needed to promote these high paying offers.

My suggestion is, start creating a real "education" blog to have some credibility and traffic before you apply for CPA approval.

You can join a CPA network at www.peerflynet.com.

I hope that you can now see how you can be making money with niche marketing — superb for AdSense, but also there are so many other options to monetize.

Do choose an "evergreen" niche market so that it can continue to generate income for you in times to come. For instance, education is an "evergreen" niche; not a trendy niche that will be here today and gone tomorrow.

Next, choose a niche that can be developed into sub-niches. The education niche is like an absolutely huge umbrella that holds so many great sub-niches under it. If you are looking for a niche that produces steady income month after month, you can't go wrong with the education niche (this is just an example).

Lastly, the biggest thing is to get into the minds of your readers. What do they want to know about?

Once you get started thinking about your target audience in that way, you'll begin to look at this niche and other broad niches in a whole new light.

72. HOW LONG CAN YOU STAND?

A while ago, I fell sick. Then my staff also fell sick. I guess it must have been the weather.

So I ended up doing a lot of work that day myself... and those were not money-making activities. They were just work!

While replying to tons of emails that day, among other things, a thought came to me... which I am going to share with you now.

"How long can you stand?"

How long can you continue to reply to emails, read more eBooks, surf the internet, read other marketers' sales letters, create your own content, submit articles, generate keywords, etc. if you don't know what you are trying to achieve?

I mean, can you do that for 7 days a week?

The truth is, it won't be possible for you to complete everything on your own. If you can, I would like to hear how you do it because I will definitely want to learn from you!

If you are not "suffering" from any of these tasks, you won't know how much time and energy it takes to "eat" you up. The next thing you know, you have become an "employee" to your online business.

I would not be surprised if you should win the "employee of the month" award if there were such an award!

For instance, my (who????) was sick and she could not do anything that day. She definitely needed a good rest.

But what if I had fallen sick as well that time?

I was reading a book by Michael Gerber called The e-Myth, in which he teaches business owners how to build a successful, small business and stay happy.

Don't get me wrong -- I am not saying that I am unhappy or anything. In fact, I am very happy with all of my online businesses today that are generating more money than I could have imagined possible.

Read that book. It contains good stuff. He teaches about systematizing a small business so that the business owner does not get "drowned" in it.

The fact is, most gurus teach about creating a "system" for your online business. Everybody understands that. Ideally, that is what you should be focusing on--every day.

What you need to do now is to stop "doing" anything related to making money online. Yes, stop writing that darn article that you have been trying to complete for the past few hours.

What I want you to do (for your own good) is to think: "Am I doing this to help me make money online?"

Many years ago, Stephen Pierce, another internet marketing friend of mine, taught me about creating a "brand" for myself. From that one idea, all of my online business is just to enhance that brand and revolve around it. Anything that is not directly related will be of secondary priority.

So if your goal is to achieve a certain result by the end of your dateline, are you doing what you can today and tomorrow to reach that?

Let's say you don't have a website yet ... should you be learning how to get traffic right now?

This question is very subjective of course.

Some may say yes because it is going to help them when the time is "right".

Great. So if you know when is the "right" time, like when your webpage will be up and running, I have no argument that you should start learning about traffic generation this instant. But if you don't even know how to buy a domain name

yet, don't you think that the better immediate action should be focusing on how to set up your website first?

Lesson learned... don't get distracted too much. A little bit is fine. No one is perfect. You and I will get distracted along the way.

Let me stretch you a bit more.

You see, any tasks going on could be affecting the way how you work towards your goal. A common "distraction" (and opportunity) is evaluating offers to promote. For instance, do you get emails requesting to do joint ventures with other marketers? Well, to make a good decision on whether to partner up or not, just ask yourself this: "Will my participation in this JV help me to move closer to achieving my *own goals?"*

Yes, really, it is that simple.

Does that makes you a bad person because you are just thinking about your own goals? Not really. I want to achieve my own goals first so I can spend more time with my ageing parents and growing kids. I want to be by my wife's side each time she laughs and cheers. I want to waste time watching movies. I want to sit by the beach reading my favorite books. I want to do so many things including offering my time to help those who need my help -- but I won't be able to do any of these if my financial goals are not achieved yet.

So I think it is okay for everyone to consider focusing on his or her own goals first ... instead of going around being a "busybody" doing things that are of much lesser worth.

Your time is very valuable. Spend it wisely to be super effective. Use the following tips to start "creating" more time for you and your online business.

1. Delegate those tasks which others can do as well as you or better. Like, packaging a product to be shipped out. Now, can others do that? You bet. Little things like these will save you a lot of time in the long run.

2. Stay focused on what you are trying to achieve from your online business. If your goal is to build a website that will rank #1 in Google for the keywords "frog jumping competition", I suggest you start focusing on building that website and learn all you can about search engines. Temporarily forget about other courses that are unrelated to it, like affiliate marketing, email marketing, copywriting, etc.

3. Think first before you do anything. Are you doing what you are supposed to do, or are you just avoiding the things you dislike?

4. If possible, follow a proven system to achieve your goal. Anthony Robbins once said, "Success leave clues." Pick up the clues from courses, people, books, audios, etc.

5. Don't fall sick. Just kidding. You can't stop the act of nature. *But you can sure prevent it to a great extent.* Stay healthy by doing healthy stuff*. Basically, eat good food, do some proper exercise, and when you have some extra budget, buy and eat some quality health supplements. And do these things every day, not just when you have the mood to do them.

I just realized I have "spent" 37 minutes on writing this chapter! It probably won't make me wealthier. But that is fine because I have probably helped you become more successful in your life and online business.

So you see, you don't have to be rigid all the time. It is fine to do the things that your heart tells you. Listen to "him" or "her". Listen to him/her more and you will discover that he/she is as smart -- maybe smarter than your brain.

* Health is very important for me. If you would like to know what do I eat to stay healthy, I'll share with you – go to:

www.patricchan.net/optimalhealth

CONCLUSION

I hope you have gained a lot of ideas and information from what you have read. In summarizing everything that I have shared on making money online ...

Before you step into the unknown world of internet marketing, make sure you get your *business mindset* and *positive attitude* ready. Learning the "how to" is just one part of the journey; you also need to think, believe and be tenacious like a real business owner and a real winner. Real business owners and winners don't quit, and they sure don't whine and blame others when things get tough -- they just get better and take another step forward.

It is really important to build an online business in a profitable niche market. Miss this and you will be like a dog chasing its own tail -- you will fail miserably. If you get on the long tail, better still.

You make money by either promoting your own product or affiliate program. If it is yours, go for digital info-products for maximum profit and automation. Whatever you are promoting online, your main focus is to solve *other people's problems* since that is what they will be motivated to pay for.

There are several ways of getting traffic to your website. Some of them shared here include building your own affiliate program, Google Adwords advertising, social media and joint venture marketing. But don't discard others not revealed here. Go and look for more to see what best suits your style.

Just selling products online won't make you rich. What will assure you a consistent income is building your own subscriber or customer database. I call this list marketing.

Building a profitable online business is not a one-time thingy. I have seen marketers come and go like nobody's business in this industry. It takes real understanding of business, discipline and whatever you can think of to make you become the best of what you are capable.

I am going to end this book with what I started in the Introduction…

After reading this book, I want you to be clear about 2 things:

The first one is you won't make a single cent online if you don't apply what you read. I know that discovering new money-making information is fun and exciting but doing them is what sets you apart from the other readers.

The second point is this: internet marketing is definitely an ongoing education. This book alone will not give you all of the information you need. Come on, be real. As a matter of fact, I am still learning! I think I spend more money now learning compared to before I started making money online. This sounds ironic, doesn't it? Not really. Here is why -- because I already know how to create income from the internet, I would make more each time I improve my knowledge and apply new internet marketing techniques I have never used before!

Wait.

There is actually one more favor if you don't mind.

If you like what you have read or gained value from it, I would appreciate tremendously if you can drop me an email with a testimonial or feedback. Please do this for me by going to:

www.patricchan.net/feedback

Thank you and best wishes!

Your friend,

Patric Chan
Best-Selling Author

FREE UNADVERTISED BONUS FOR MY BOOK READERS:

Congratulation for completing the book. Most people never reach this page. ☺ Therefore, as a reward for your determination to succeed, I've prepared a free gift for you, redeem it at:

www.patricchan.net/congrats

Or scan below:

Made in the USA
Middletown, DE
23 May 2019